Early A
Cookery
or
Ye Gentlewoman's
Housewifery

CONTAINING

Scarce, Curious, and *Valuable Receipts*
For making ready all forts of Viands

A REPOSITORY of USEFUL KNOWLEDGE
Adapted to meet the wants of
GOOD WIVES AND TENDER MOTHERS

ALSO

Sundry Salutory Remedies of Sovereign
and Approved Efficacy

And

Choice Secrets on the Improvement
of Female Beauty

COMPILED FROM OLD AND RELIABLE SOURCES

By
MARGARET HUNTINGTON HOOKER

©2010 Native Ground Books & Music
Asheville, N. C. International Copyright Secured.
All Rights Reserved. Order Number: NGB-840
ISBN:9781883206505
Library of Congress Control Number: 2010920610
www.nativeground.com

Telling the Bees.

Introduction to the 2010 Edition

Margaret Huntington Hooker's intriguing book was first published in 1896 under the title *Ye Gentlewoman's Housewifery*. Precious little is known about the author. We do know that she was born in 1868 in Rochester, New York, and was one of the six children of Horace and Susan Huntington Hooker. Margaret was an eighth generation descendant of the Rev. Thomas Hooker, one of the founders of Connecticut. In 1909, she edited a 558 page book of genealogy of the Hooker family entitled *Descendants of the Rev. Thomas Hooker.*

Margaret's father ran a nursery, owned a shoe factory, and operated a successful general contracting business. The Hooker family owned a second home in the village of Mandarin, Florida, where they often spent their winters. Unlike her brothers who followed scientific and business careers, Margaret had a strong aptitude for art, weaving, book making, cooking and history. She published *Ye Gentlewoman's House-wifery* when she was 28 years of age. Three years later, in 1899, she attended Vassar College for one year and then studied at the Art Students League in New York City. She died in 1936 at the age 68.

As you'll discover as you look through this book of colonial American cookery, the author used what is generally referred to as the "long S script," which was popular in the 18th century with publishers such as Benjamin Franklin.

In many ways, Margaret Huntington Hooker's book is a fascinating historic document in itself. When she compiled her book of colonial cookery at the close of the 19th century, she included recipes which were written one hundred to one hundred and fifty years earlier. She chose tasty as well as quirky old "receipts," and then threw in a few favorites from her own era. Though Margaret did not document her sources, food historian Kay Moss of the Schiele Museum of Natural History in Gastonia, North Carolina, has traced the roots of many of Hooker's recipes:

The Art of Cookery Made Plain and
        Easy, Hannah Glasse, 1747
The Compleat Housewife, Eliza Smith, 1758
American Cookery, Amelia Simmons, 1796
The American Frugal Housewife,
        Lydia Child, 1833
Primitive Physick, John Wesley, 1791
Every Man His Own Doctor, John Tennent, 1736

We hope you enjoy this culinary trip back in time as seen through the late-19th century eyes of a young Margaret Huntington Hooker.

Wayne Erbsen, Asheville, North Carolina
January 1st, 2010

Preface.

—◆—

THE difcerning Reader will fee at once
that in this little book it has been my
Intention to Prefent for the Edification
of the Amiable Sex, a curfory glance at
the table plenifhings and Domeftic cuf-
toms of our Forebears in this country;
Not only of thofe whofe Fortune it was
to partake of the delectable Repafts ferved
at the tables of the Opulent, but alfo of
thofe lefs favored families, whofe homely
Fare preferved the mean between Prodi-
gality and Parfimony.

Some of thefe Recipes have been col-
lected from quaint family Manufcripts,
contributed by ancient Ladies, whofe
affurances of fupport and teftimonials of
Approbation have cheered not a little the
                                        tafk

tafk of Accumulation. Others have been gathered from old and efteemed printed Works, often so fraught with extravagant Recipes and full of odd and fantaftic Meffes, meant only for the palate of the Gourmand, that the tafk of Selection has been one of exceeding Perplexity.

It has not been my Endeavor to write thefe Recipes in a high polite Style, but rather to keep intact the choice Diction of thofe with whom they Originated, and to prefent thofe which illuftrate in fome Fafhion or other the Characteriftics of the laft Century, and that part of this previous to the general Introduction of that Modern Abomination — an iron Cook-ftove.

The Faultfinder — who perchance " never fhook hands with a Stewpan " — may fay that I have too often trefpaffed into Englifh fields. Thofe who have exercifed their underftanding know of the Paucity of early gaftronomic Literature in this Country, and how many a female Manager, circumfcribed in her Knowledge, hailed with joy the reprint of an
Englifh

Englifh book, adapted to the Wants and Requirements of the American Publick.

If the Skeptic requires further evidence of the Efteem in which one of the moft popular of Englifh books was held, let me quote for his Enlightenment from a Book on American Cookery publifhed early in the Century.

" Mrs. Hannah Glafs — who hath done more for the happinefs of mankind than all the blue ftockings of this or any other age, There is fcarcely a civilized being who hath not been benefited by her labours in the caufe of human happinefs, and it is one of the indications of a bafe ungrateful world that neither ftatue nor monument, nay, not even a biography or a pudding hath been confecrated to her memory — Mrs. Glafs's unparalleled genius as fur outfhines and overtops that of Mrs. Hemans and other female venders of empty poetry, as doth a white fricaffee or a difh of buttered eggs exceed the frothy evaporations of a brain moiftened by the dews of Parnaffus. What comparifon can there be between the falfe
fentiment

fentiment and flimfy philofophy of Madame de Stael and the folid puddings of Mrs. Glafs? Talk of an Epic poem! Verily, gentle reader, it is little better than downright nonfenfe. There are the Iliad, the Odyffey, the Aeneid, the Pharfalia, the Argonaut, the Jerufalem Delivered, the Paradife Loft, the Henriade, and the Vifion of Columber. But there is only one plum pudding and one Mrs. Glafs!"

This Excurfion into the "affairs of the mouth" of long ago is prefented with fome Reluctancy in the melancholy profpect that a Critical Publick may expect to find an exhauftive Differtation on the Culinary art and its Appurtenances, where only Houfewifely hints and fome curiofities of old time practice have been given.

If perchance fome portions of the Recipes prove in practice not altogether a grievous Penance to modern organs of Tafte, and others Contribute fomewhat to the entertainment of our fair Patroneffes the labour will not have been in Vain.

I

I wifh to acknowledge my obligation to thofe who have fo kindly brought forth family heirlooms, to illuftrate thefe pages, and efpecially to the Deerfield Memorial Hall with its rare treafures, the American Antiquarian Society, Worcefter Society of Antiquity, Concord Antiquarian Society, Connecticut Hiftorical Society and the Long Ifland Hiftorical Society.

Contents.

———

List of Illustrations.

Hobnobbing in 1800.

Yᵉ Gentlewoman's Housewifery.

SOUPS AND SAUCES.

Of Soups.

Obſerva- No good Houſewife has any
tion.   pretenſions to Rational Econ-
omy who boils Animal Food without
converting the Broth into ſome ſort of
Soup.

Hotch-Potch Take a Neck of Mutton of
of Mutton. about ſix pounds, and cut it
into Chops. Leave the ſcrag-end Whole.
Put it into a Bag with half a pint of Water ;
ſweat it gently over a Stewpan with half a

pint

pint of Water. Put in fix round Onions and fix middle-fized Turnips whole, a Carrot cut in Quarters, a favoy or white cabbage cut in quarters and tied up with pack Thread all well wafhed, with a little Thyme; fweat it gently for half an Hour, then pour three quarts of boiling Water over it, Seafon it with Salt and Pepper, and fkim it Well. Stew it for two hours, fkim off all the Fat, put the Chops into a Soup Difh, leave out the Scrag, untie the Cabbage put over with the Soup. Garnifh with toafted Sippets. Add two ounces of Scotch Barley if you like it.

Afparagus Soup. Take twelve Pounds of lean Beef cut in Slices, then put a Quarter of a pound of Butter in a Stewpan over the Fire, and put your Beef in. Let it boil up quick till it begins to brown, then put in a Pint of Brown Ale

2   and

and a Gallon of Water, cover it clofe, and let it Stew gently for an hour and a half. Put in what Spice you like in the Stewing. Strain out the Liquor, Skim off the Fat, then put in fome Vermecelly and Afparagus cut fmall and Potatoes boiled tender and cut. Put all thefe in, and Boil gently until Tender.

Just as it's going up, Fry a Handful of Spinage in Butter, and throw in a French Roll.

Soup of Lambs Head and Pluck. Put the Head, Heart and Lights, with one pound Pork into five quarts of Water. After boiling one Hour add Liver. Add alfo Potatoes, Carrots, Onions, Parfley, Summer Savory and Sweet Marjoram. Take half pound of Butter worked into one pound of Flour a fmall quantity of Summer Savory Pepper and two Eggs, work well together, make into fmall Balls, and drop in Soup while Hot. Now ferve it up.

A

A Pepper-pot. To three quarts of Water, put fuch Vegetables as you choofe, — in Summer, Peas, Lettuce, Spinach and two or three Onions, in Winter, Carrot, Turnip, Onions and Celery. Cut them in Bits, and ftew them with two pounds of Neck of Mutton and a pound of Pickled Pork, till quite tender. Half an hour before ferving clear a Lobfter from the fhell, and put it into the Stew. Some People choofe very fmall Suet Dumplings boiled in the above. Seafon with Salt and Cayenne.

Inftead of Mutton you may put Fowl. Pepper-pot may be made of various Things, and is underftood to be a proper mixture of Fifh, Flefh, Fowl, Vegetables and Pulfe. A fmall quantity of Rice fhould be boiled with the Whole.

Portable Soup. Let Veal or Beef Soup get quite cold, then fkim off every Particle of the Fat, boil it till of a thick Glutinous confiftence. Care fhould be

4 taken

taken not to have the Soup Burn. Season it very Highly with Pepper, Salt, Cloves and Mace; add a little Brandy, and pour it over earthen Platters not more than a quarter of an inch in Thicknefs. Let it be till Cold, then cut it in three-inch Square pieces, fet them in the Sun to Dry, often turning them. When very Dry place them in a Earthen Veffel, having a layer of White Paper between each layer of Cakes. Thefe will keep good for a long time and will be found very Convenient for thofe whom travel or bufinefs compels to dine haftily. They form an Extemporaneous difh of the moft Nutritious order.

A Family Take a Piece of Butter rolled
Cullis. in Flour, and Stir it in your Stewpan till your Flour is of a yellow Color; then put in fome Fine Broth a little Gravy, a Glafs of White Wine, a Bundle of Parfley, Thyme, Laurel and

Sweet

Sweet Bafil, two Cloves, a little Nutmeg or Mace, a few Mufhrooms and Pepper and Salt. Let it ftew an Hour over a Slow Fire; cover clofe. Then fkim all the Fat clean off and Strain through a Lawn Sieve.

To Make Peas-Porridge. Take a Quart of Green Peas, put them to a Quart of Water, a Bundle of dried Mint and a little Fat; boil till tender, then put in fome beaten Pepper a Piece of Butter rolled in Flour. Stir it, let it Boil, then add two Quarts of Milk, boil, take out the Mint, and ferve up.

Cock-a-leekie. Boil from four to fix Pounds of good Shin-beef, well broken till the Liquor is very good. Strain it, and put to it a Capon or large Fowl, trussed for boiling, and, when it boils, half the Quantity of Blanched Leeks intended to be ufed, well cleaned and cut in Inch Lengths or longer. Skim this carefully.

6   In

In a Half-hour add the remaining Part of the Leeks, and the firft Part will be boiled down into Soup, till it becomes a Green lubricious Compound.

This is a good Leek-foup without the Fowl.

Of Sauces.

Obferva- " Muftard is meete for Brawn,
tion.   Beef or powdred Mouton, Perdins to boyled Capoun, Veel, Chicken or Bakoun Rooft Beeff and Goos with Garlek, Vineger or Peper Gynger Sawce to Lambe, to Kyd, Pigge, or Fawn. To Phyfand, Partriche or Cony, Muftard with the Sugure."

Boke of Nurture.

Tomatas Thefe have gone down in
or Love France, but are juft coming
Apples. in Vogue in other Countrys. They are ufed in Soups and Sauces and are pickled. Some People hitherto have thought them only Ornamental or of a Poifonous Nature, but they are a delectable Addition to our Aliments.

     Tomata

Tomata Sauce. Take from Ten to Fifteen ripe Tomatas or fewer according to their Size, put in a Jar and set on the Hot hearth. When they are foft take off the Skins, pick out the Seeds, and mix the Pulp with a Capficum, a Clove of Garlic and a very little Vinegar, Ginger, Cayenne, White Pepper and Salt. Pulp this through a Sieve, and fimmer it for a few Minutes. Beet root Juice is

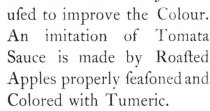

ufed to improve the Colour. An imitation of Tomata Sauce is made by Roafted Apples properly feafoned and Colored with Tumeric.

Note. In this Sauce French Cooks ftew Onion, a Piece of Ham, a Sprig of Thyme, a Bay leaf, and ufe Top Fat or a rich Cullis to moiften the Ingredients. Good Practice.

Pap Sauce for Venifon. Grate white Bread, and boil it with Port Wine, Water and large Stick of Cinnamon; when fmooth take out Cinnamon, and add Sugar.

8 *Effence*

Effence of Ham. Take Three Pounds of lean Ham, and cut it into Pieces about an Inch thick. Lay them in the Bottom of a Stew-pan, with Slices of Carrots, Parfnips, and three or four Onions cut thin. Let them ftew till they ftick to the Pan, but do not let them burn. Then pour on fome ftrong Veal Gravy by degrees, fome frefh Mufh-rooms cut in Pieces, (but if not to be had, Mufhroom Powder) Truffles and Morels, Cloves, Bafil, Parfley, a cruft of bread, and a Leek. Cover it down Clofe, and when it has fimmered till it is of a good Thicknefs  and flavour, ftrain it off. If you have preferved the Gravy from a drefled Ham, you may ufe it with the before-mentioned Ingredients, inftead of the Ham, which will make it equally good, but not quite fo high Flavoured.

Afpic Sauce. Infufe Chervil, Tarragon, Bur-net Garden Crefs and Mint,

9   into

into a little Cullis for about half an Hour, or until it is as good as you want it ; then ſtrain it, and add a Spoonful of Garlic-Vinegar with a little Pepper and Salt.

Walnut Ketchup of the Fineſt Sort. Boil or ſimmer a Gallon of the expreſſed Juice of Walnuts when they are tender, and ſkim it well; then put in two Pounds of Anchovies' Bones and Liquor, ditto of Shallots, one Ounce of Cloves, Mace, Pepper and one Clove of Garlic. Let all ſimmer till the Shallots ſink. When cold bottle. Cork Cloſe, and tie a bladder over. Will keep 20 Years.

Bill-Berries or Whortle-Berries. A moſt excellent Summer Diſh. They uſually eat of them put in a Baſon with Milk and Sweetened a little more with Sugar and Spice, or for Cold Stomachs in Sack. When dryed they uſe them inſtead of Currence, putting of them into Puddens, both boyled and baked and into Water Gruel.

Vingaret

Vingaret for Cold Fowl or Meat. Chop Mint, Parſley and Shallot. Mix with Salt, Oil, and Vinegar. Serve in a Boat.

A pretty little Sauce. Take the Liver of the Fowl, bruiſe it with a little of the Liquor, melt ſome good butter, cut a little Lemon peel fine, and mix with the Liver by degrees ; give it a boil, and pour it into the diſh.

Carrier Sauce for Mutton. Take ſeven Spoonfuls of Spring Water, Slice two Onions of moderate Size into a large Saucer, and put in as much Salt as you can hold at thrice betwixt your Fore-finger and Thumb if large, and serve up.

Fennel Sauce. Boil a Bunch of Fennel and Parſley, Chop it very ſmall, and Stir it into ſome melted Butter.

Cranberry

Cran-Berry or Bear-Berry Sauce. The Indians and Englifh eat them much, boyling them with Sugar to eat with their meat,

and it is a delicate Sauce, efpecially for roafted Mutton. Some make Tarts with them.

They are alfo good to allay the fervour of hot Difeafes.

Pompian Sauce. Ancient New England Standing-difh. The Houfewives' Manner is to Slice them when ripe and cut them into Dice, and fo fill a Pot with them of two or three Gallons, and ftew them upon a gentle Fire the whole Day. And as they fink fill again with frefh Pompians, not putting any Liquor to them, and when it is ftirred enough it will look like bak'd Apples. This they Difh putting Butter to and a little Vinegar with fome Spice as Ginger which makes it tart like an Apple, and ferve it up to be eaten with Fifh or Flefh.

Apple

Apple Sauce for Goose and Roast Pork. Pare, Core and Slice fome Apples and put them in a ftone Jar into a Saucepan of Water, or on a hot Hearth. If on a Hearth, let a Spoonful or two of Water be put in to hinder from burning. When they are done bruife them to a Mafh.

Add a little brown Sugar. Serve in a Sauce-tureen.

Waffle Gravy. As Waffles are rather hard and dry when baked, they are improved by the following Sauce. Boil a Pint of Milk, take it from the Fire, and ftir in a Teafpoonful of Salt and half a Cup of Butter. When the Butter is melted and ftirred in with the Milk, it is ready to ferve with the Waffles.

To Collar Take your
Eels. Eels and
Scour well with Salt,
wipe it clean; then cut
it down the Back, take
out the Bone, cut the
Head and Tail off.
Put the Yolk of an
Egg over it and then
take four Cloves, two
Blades of Mace, half
a Nutmeg beat fine,
a little Pepper and
Sweet Herbs chopped
very fine. Mix them
all together and Sprin-
kle over it. Roll the
Eel up very tight and
tie it in a Cloth ; Put
on Water enough to
Boil it, and put in an
Onion, some Cloves
and Mace, four Bay-
leaves. Boil it up with
the Bones, Head and
14   Tail

Tail for half an Hour with a little Salt and Vinegar; then take out the Bones and fo forth, and put in your Eels. Boil them, if large, two Hours, leffer in Proportion. When done put them away to cool. Then take them out of the Liquor and Cloth and cut them in Slices or fend them Whole, with raw Parfley under and over.

To Pitch- Take a large Eel, and fcour
cock Eels. it well with Salt to clean off
all the Slime;
then flit it down
the Back, take
out the Bone, and cut it in three or four pieces; take the Yolk of an Egg and put over the Infide, fprinkle Crumbs of Bread with fome fweet Herbs and Parfley chopped very fine, a little Nutmeg grated, and fome Pepper and Salt, mixed all together; then put it on a Grid-iron over a clear fire,
broil it to a fine
light Brown, difh it up, and garnifh with raw Parfley and Horfe-radifh; or put

a boiled Eel in the middle and the Pitchcocked round. Garniſh as above with Anchovy-ſauce, and Parſley and Butter in a Boat.

Cod's Sounds to look like Small Chickens. This is a good Maigre-day Diſh. Waſh three large Sounds nicely and boil in Milk and Water but not too tender. When cold put forcemeat of Chopped Oyſters, Crumbs of Bread, a Bit of Butter, Nutmeg, Pepper, Salt and the Yolks of two Eggs. Spread it thin over the Sounds, then roll up each in the Form of Chickens, Skewering it; then

lard them as you would Chicken, duſt a little Flour over them and roaſt them in a tin Oven ſlowly. When done pour over them a fine Oyſter Sauce and Serve as a Side or Corner Diſh.

Roaſt Lobſter. We give no Receipt for Roaſt Lobſter, being of the Opinion with Dr. King who ſays : —

16   " By

" By Roafting that which our Fore-
fathers Boiled and Boiling what they
Roafted, much is Spoiled."

A Codfiſh   Take thin Slivers of Cod-
Reliſh.   fifh, lay them on hot Coals
and when a yellowifh brown, fet them on
the Table.

To dreſs   Lay them in Water all Night
Cod's   and then boil them ; if they
Zoons.   be Salt fhift them once in the
boiling ; when they are tender cut them
in long Pieces ; drefs them up with Eggs
as you do Salt-fifh ; take
one or two of them and
cut into fquare Pieces; dip
them in Egg, and fry them
to lay round your Difh.
    It is proper to lay
round any other Difh.

To Butter   Stew a Quart of Shrimps
Shrimps.   with half a Pint of White-
wine, with Nutmeg ; then beat four
Eggs with a little White-wine, and a
Quarter of a Pound of beaten Butter;

2   17   then

then fhake them well in a Difh till they
be thick enough, then ferve them up
with one Sippet for a Side difh.

Stewed   Put the Oyfters into a Sieve
Oyfters.   and fet it on a Pan to drain the
Liquor from them.   Then cut off the
hard Part and put the Oyfters into a
Stew-pan with fome whole Pepper, a few
blades of Mace, and fome grated Nutmeg.   Add a fmall Piece of Butter rolled
in Flour.   Then pour over them about
half the Liquor or a little more.   Set
the pan upon hot Coals and fimmer
about five minutes.   Try one, and if it
taftes raw, cook them a little longer.
Make fome thin Slices of Toaft, having

cut off all the Cruft,
Butter the Toaft and
lay it in the Bottom of
a deep Difh.   Put the
Oyfters upon it with
the Liquor in which they were Stewed.

Oyfter   Make a Hole in the Top of
Loaves.   fome little round Loaves, and
take out all the Crumbs.   Put fome

Oyfters

Oyſters into a Stew-pan, with Oyſter liquor, and the Crumbs that were taken out of the Loaves, and a large Piece of Butter ; ſtew them together five or ſix Minutes, then put in a Spoonful of good Cream, then fill your Loaves. Lay a bit of Cruſt carefully on the Top of each, and put them in the Oven to criſp.

Pickled Oyſters. Take a Quart of Oyſters and waſh them in their own Liquor very well till all grittineſs is out, put them in a Stew-pan, Strain the Liquor over them and ſet  them on the Fire and ſcum them. Then put in three or four Blades of Mace, a Spoonful of whole Pepper-corns ; when you think they are enough ; it will take about five Minutes ; throw in a glaſs of White-wine. Let them have a thorough Scald, then take out. Take them up, put them in a Pot, boil up the Pickle, ſcum it, and pour it over them.

Caveach

Caveach or pickled Mackerel. Take half a Dozen of large Mackerel and cut them into round Pieces. Then take an Ounce of beaten Pepper, three large Nutmegs, a little Mace and a Handful of Salt. Mix your Salt and beaten Spice, make two or three Holes in each Piece and thruft the Seafoning into the Holes. Rub them over with the Seafoning, fry them brown in Oil, when Cold Cover them with Vinegar and pour Oil on the top. They make a fine Mefs for Supper.

To drefs a Turtle. You must firft cut off the Turtle's Head, then cut it all around and part the two Shells as you do a Crab, but take Care that fome Meat be left on the Breaft-fhell which is called the Cullupy, and feafon it with Butter, Pepper, Spice and put fome Forced-meat Balls between the Flefh, and with fome Meat with it. Bake and bafte it with Madeira Wine and Butter. Then from the deep Shell called the Callabafh, take out all the Meat and the Intrails, except

the

the Monfieur, which is the Fat and
looks green, that muft be left in and
baked with the Shell : and with a Pen-
knife open every Gut, and Clean them
well and cut them an Inch and a half
long or two Inches as you think fit,
and cut the other Meat into Quarters
of Pound Pieces. You muft clean the
Fins as you do Goofe Giblets and cut
them into Pieces, Stew the Fins and
Meat together till tender — an Hour
will do it — and then Strain it off,
thicken your Soup, and put all your
Meat and Guts in
it as you do Goofe
Giblets, Seafon it
with Cayan, But-
ter, Pepper, Spice,
Salt, Shallots, Sweet herbs and Madeira
Wine to your Liking, and put it all into
the deep Shell. Send it to the oven to
bake and Serve it up.

To make Take fome of the fmalleft
Water- Plaice or Flounders you can
Sokey. get, wafh them clean, cut the

Fins close, put them into a Stew-pan, with juft Water enough to boil them, a  little Salt, and a Bunch of Parfley ; when they are cooked enough fend them to Table in a Soup-difh, with the Liquor to keep them hot ; have Parfley and But-ter in a Cup.

Eals in a Stuff the Eals with Nutmegs
Wreath. and Cloves, Cook them in Wine, place on a Chafing Difh in a Wreath, and garnifh with Lemon.

Rules to be observed in roasting Meat, Poultry and Game.

I fhall give the moft modern Fafhions and muft defire the Cook to order her Fire according to what fhe has to drefs : if Anything very little or thin, then a pretty little brifk Fire, that it may be done quick and nice ; if a very large Joint, then be Sure a good Fire be laid

to

to Cake. Let it be clear at the bottom : and when your Meat is half done move the Dripping-pan and Spit a little from the Fire and Stir up a good brisk Fire : for according to the Goodnefs of your Fire, your Meat will be done fooner or later. Take great Care the Spit be very clean, and be fure and clean it with nothing but Sand and Water, wafh it clean and wipe it with a dry Cloth : for Oil, Brick-duft and Such things will Spoil your Meat.

To Roaft Beef. Never roaft a Piece of Beef in the Oven. No Meat is fo much injured as Beef by roafting in an Oven. Sprinkle Salt upon the Beef when it is put upon the Spit, and rub it in with your Hand, then dredge it with Flour, put Water into the Pan with a little Salt, and place the whole before a moderate Fire for Fifteen or twenty Minutes, turning every Part to the Fire in

order

order that the Salt and Flour may be incorporated with the Juices of the Meat; then quicken your Fire and place the Beef clofe before it; as faft as the Beef browns, bafte and dredge it, turning the Spit as often as neceffary until the Meat is cooked.

To broil Beef Steaks. Take your Beef Steaks and beat them with the Back of a Knife, ftrew them over with a

little Pepper, and Salt, lay them on a Gridiron over a clear Fire, turning them till they are enough; fet your Difh over a Chafing-difh of Coals, with a little brown Gravy; chop an Onion fmall and put it among the Gravy (if your Steak be not over much done, Gravy will come therefrom), put it on a Difh and fhake it together. Garnifh your Difh with Shalots and Pickles.

To fry Tripe. Cut your Tripe in long Pieces about three inches wide, and

all

all the Breadth of the Double, put it in
fome fmall Beer and the Yolks of Eggs ;
Have a large Pan of good Fat, and fry
it brown, then take it out and put it to
drain.

Dean Swift's Receipt for Roaft Mutton.

Gently Stir and blow the Fire
Lay the Mutton down to roaft.
Drefs it quickly, I defire,
In the Dripping put a Toaft,
That I hunger may remove
Mutton is the Meat I love.

In the Dreffer fee it lie ;
Oh ! the charming White and Red;
Finer Meat ne'er
    met the eye,
On the fweetelt
    grafs it fed :
Let the Jack go fwiftly round
Let me have it nicely browned.

On the Table fpread the Cloth
Let the Knives be fharp and clean
Pickles get and Salad both

Let

Let them each be frefh and green.
With fmall Beer, good Ale, and Wine
Oh ve Gods! How I fhall dine!

Veal   Slice your Veal, lard it with
Cutlets. Bacon, feafon with Nutmeg,
Pepper, Salt, Lemon-thyme and fweet
Marjoram, wafh them with Eggs firft,
Strew over the Seafoning, dip them
in melted Butter and wrap them in
buttered white Paper. Then broil them
on a Gridiron fome diftance from the
Fire. When done enough, take off the
Paper, ferve with Gravy, garnifh with
fliced Lemon.

Various   Firft Skin your Pig up to the
Ways of Ears whole, then make a good
dreffing Plumb Pudding Batter, with
a Pig.   good beef Fat, Fruit, Eggs,
Milk and Flour; fill the Skin and Sew
it up; it will look like a Pig; but you
muft bake it, flour it very well, and rub
it all over with Butter, and when it is
near enough, draw it to the Oven's
mouth, rub it dry, and put it in again
for a few Minutes; lay it in the Difh,

and let the Sauce be fmall
Gravy and Butter in the Difh ;
cut the other Part of the Pig
into four Quarters, roaft them
as you do Lamb, throw Mint
and Parfley on it as it roafts ;
then lay them on Water-
creffes, and have Mint Sauce
in a Bafon. Any one of thefe
Quarters will make a pretty
Side-difh : or take one Quarter and roaft, cut the Other
in Steaks, and fry them fine
and brown. Have ftewed
Spinage in the Difh, and lay
the Roaft upon it, and the
Fried in the Middle. Gar-
nifh with hard Eggs and
Seville Oranges cut into
Quarters, and have fome
Butter in a Cup ; or for
Change, you may have good
gravy in the difh, and garnifh
with fried Parfley and Lemon ; or you may make a
Ragoo of Sweetbreads, Arti-

27   choke

choke Bottoms, Truffles, Morels, and good Gravy, and pour over them. Garnifh with Lemon. Either of thefe will do for a Top-difh of a firft Courfe. You may fricaffee it white for a fecond Courfe at Top, or a Side-difh.

You may take a Pig, fkin him and fill him with Force-meat thus : take two Pounds of young Pork, fat and all, two Pounds of Veal the fame, fome Sage, Thyme, Parfley, a little Lemon-peel, Pepper, Salt, Mace, Cloves, and a Nutmeg : mix them and beat them fine in a Mortar, then fill the Pig, and Sew it up. You may either roaft or bake it. Have Nothing but good Gravy in the Difh.

Venifon. Should be rather under than overdone. Spread a Sheet of Paper with Butter and put it over the Fat, firft fprinkle it with Salt, then lay a coarfe Pafte on ftrong Paper and cover the haunch; tie it with fine Pack thread, and fet it at Diftance from the Fire which muft be a good One. Bafte it often; ten minutes before ferving, take off Pafte,

draw

draw Meat nearer Fire, and bafte with Butter and a good deal of Flour to make froth up well. Garnifh Knuckle-bone with Ruffle of cut Writing Paper. Pap Sauce is eaten with venifon.

The Ufeful and Polite Art of Carving. I am fure that Poets as well as Cooks are for having Words nicely chofen, and muft regret to hear fome Perfons of Quality fay, " Pray cut up that Goofe, Help me to fome of that Chicken, Hen, or Capon," or " Halve that Plover," not confidering how indif- creetly they talk before Men of Art, whofe proper Terms are " Break that Goofe," " Fruft that Chicken," " Spoil that Hen," " Sauce that Capon," " Mince that Plover." If they are fo much out in common Things how much more will they be with Herons, Cranes and Peacocks.

To Cut up a Turkey. Raife up the Leg fairly, and open the Joint with the Point of your Knife, but take not off the Leg: then with your Knife lace down

both

both Sides of the Breaſt and open the Breaſt-Pinion, but do not take it off: then raiſe the Merry-Thought betwixt the Breaſt-Bone and the Top of it: then raiſe up the Brawn: then turn it Outward upon both Sides, but break it not, nor cut it off: then cut off the Wing-Pinions at the Joint next the Body, and ſtick each Pinion in the Place you turned the Brawn out: but cut off the ſharp End of the Pinion, and take the Middle-Piece, and that will juſt Fit in its Place. You may Sauce a Capon the ſame way.

To Dreſs a Stubble Gooſe. Take a *Gooſe*, kill, and hang it up in the Feathers, two or three Nights as it ſuits you.

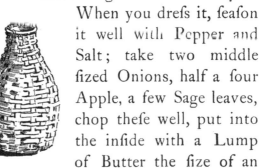

When you dreſs it, ſeaſon it well with Pepper and Salt; take two middle ſized Onions, half a ſour Apple, a few Sage leaves, chop theſe well, put into the inſide with a Lump of Butter the ſize of an Egg and a Teacup full of Water. Tie it

up

up clofe at both Ends. If a large *Goofe* it will take an Hour and a half, if a fmall One an Hour. Difh it up. Pour into your Difh fome brown Gravy with two Spoonfuls of red Wine, the fame of Ale. Serve it up with Apple Sauce.

How to Roaft a Goofe or Turkey. Take a Goofe or Turkey, and to make Stuffing for the Breaft, take Beef-fuet, the Liver fhred fine, and Bread-Crumbs, a little Lemon-peel, Nutmeg, Pepper and Salt to your Tafte, a little frefh Parfley, a Spoonful or two of Cream, and two Eggs; and as foon as you have put them to the Fire, take great Care to finge them with white Paper, and bafte them well with Butter; dredge them with a little Flour, and when the Smoke draws to the Fire, and they look plump and brown, bafte and dredge them and take them up. 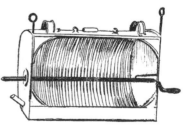 For Sauce for the Goofe,

make

make a little good Gravy, put it into a Bafon by itfelf, and Apple-fauce in another. For Turkey, fome good Gravy in the Difh, and either Bread or Onion Sauce in a Bafon. Or elfe take a little whole Pepper, let them boil well together, put a little Flour and a Lump of Butter, which you pour upon the Turkey; you may lay round your Turkey Forced-meat Balls. Garnifh your Difh with Slices of Lemon.

Celery Stuffing for Turkey. 1 coffee cup of foft Bread crumbs, 1 cup of finely chopped celery, 1 piece of onion, fize of a Walnut, chopped Fine. To this add falt, pepper, fweet Bafil, fweet Marjoram, and a large fpoonful of fweet Butter.

To Stew Ducks, either Wild or Tame. Take two Ducks, and half roaft them, cut them up as you would for eating, put them in a Stew-pan with a little brown Gravy, a Glafs of Claret, two Anchovies, a fmall Onion fhred very fine,

and a little Salt;
thicken it with
Flour and Butter,
fo ferve it up.
Garnifh your Difh with Onion Sippets.

To Stew Take three or four Breaft
Pullets. Pullets, and boil them very
tender, Blanch and cut them in long
 Pieces the Length of
your Finger, then in
fmall Bits the crofs
Way; fhake them up
with a little good Gravy
and a Lump of Butter;
feafon them with a lit-
tle Nutmeg and Salt, put in a Spoonful
of White-wine, and thicken it with the
Yolk of Eggs as you do a white Fricafey.

How Take fix or eight Pigeons,
to jug and Trufs them, feafon them
Pigeons. with Nutmeg, Pepper and Salt.
(To make the Stuffing.) Take the
Livers, and Shred them with Beef-fuet,
Bread-crumbs, Parfley, Sweet-Marjoram,

and two Eggs; Mix all together, then
Stuff your Pigeons, fewing them up at
Both ends, and put them into your Jug
with the Breafts downwards, with Half a
Pound of Butter; ftop up the Jug clofe
with a Cloth, that no fteam can get out,
then Set them in a Pot of Water to boil;
they will take about two Hours boiling;
mind you keep your Pot full of Water,
and boiling all the Time; when they are
enough,
c l e a r
f r o m
them the Gravy, and take the Fat clear
off; put to your Gravy a Spoonful of
Cream, a little Lemon-peel, an Anchovy
fhred, a few Mufhrooms, and a little
White-wine, thicken with a little Flour
and Butter, then difh your Pigeons, and
pour over them the Sauce. Garnifh the
Difh with Mufhrooms and Slices of
Lemon. This is proper for a Side-difh.

Pigeons   Take your Pigeons, feafon
Tranfmog- them with Pepper and Salt,
rified.   take a large Piece of butter,

make

make a Puff Paſte and roll each Pigeon in a Piece of Paſte ; tie them in a Cloth ſo that the Paſte does not break, boil them in a good deal of water ; they will take an hour and a half boiling, untie them Carefully that they do not break ; lay them in a diſh, and you may pour a little good Gravy in the diſh. They will eat exceeding good and nice, and will  yield ſauce enough of a very Agreeable reliſh.

To force Cock's-combs. Parboil your Cock's-combs, then open them with the point of a Knife at the great end : take the white of a Fowl, as much bacon and beef-marrow, cut theſe Small, and beat them fine in a marble mortar; Seaſon with Salt, Pepper, and grated Nutmeg, and mix it with an Egg; fill the cock's-combs, and Stew them in a little Strong gravy Softly for half an Hour; then Slice in Some freſh Muſh-

rooms

rooms and a few pickled ones ; then beat up the Yolk of an Egg in a little gravy, Stirring it. Seafon with Salt. When they are Enough, diſh them up in little Diſhes or plates.

Chickens Surpriſe. Take half a Pound of Rice, ſet it over a Fire in ſoft Water, when it is half boiled put in two or three ſmall Chickens truffed, with two or three Blades of Mace, and a little Salt ; take a Piece of Bacon about three Inches ſquare, and boil it in Water till it is almoſt enough, take it out, pare off the Outſides and put into the Chickens and Rice to boil a little together ; then take up your Chickens, lay them on a diſh, pour over them the Rice, cut your Bacon in thin Slices to lay round your Chickens, and upon the Breaſt of each a Slice. This is proper for a Side-diſh.

Of Made Dishes.

To Grill a Calves Head. Waſh your Calves head clean, and boil it almoſt enough, then take it up and haſh one half. Rub the other half with Yolk of an Egg, a little Pepper and  Salt. Strew over it bread crumbs, Parſley chopped fine, and a little grated Lemon Peel. Set it before the fire, and keep baſting it all the time to make the froth Ariſe. When it be of a light brown, diſh up your half, and lay the grilled Side upon it. Blanch your tongue, ſlit it down the middle, and lay it upon a Soup Plate. Skin the brains, boil them with a little Parſley and Sage. Chop them fine and mix them with ſome Melted butter and a Spoonful of Cream. Make them hot, and Pour them over the Tongue. Serve them up and they are ſauce for the Head.

37   *Mutton*

Mutton Take a loin of a Mutton and
Kebobbed. joint it between every bone ;
Seafon it with Pepper and
falt Moderately, grate a
fmall nutmeg all over, dip
the Chops in the yolks of
three eggs, and have ready
crumbs of Bread and fweet
Herbs, dip them in, and
Clap them together in their
former Shape again, and
put it on a fmall fpit and
roaft it before a quick Fire.

Set a difh under and bafte it
with a little piece of Butter, and with what comes
from it. Throw fome
Crumbs of bread and fweet
herbs all over it while
roafting ; When it is
enough, take it up, lay it
on a Difh, and have ready
half a pint of good Made
Gravy, and what comes
from the Mutton, take two fpoonfuls of
Catchup, and mix a tea fpoonful of Flour

with

with it, and put it to the gravy. Stir it Together, give it a boil and pour over the Mutton.

Beef   Take a brifket of Beef, bone it,
Royal. and with a Knife make holes in it about an inch from each other. Fill one hole with fat Bacon, a fecond with Parfley Chopped, and a third with chopped oyfters. Let thefe Stuffings be feafoned with Pepper, Salt, and Nutmeg.

When the beef be completely Stuffed pour upon it a pint of wine boiling hot; then dredge it well with flour, and fend it to the Oven.

Let it remain in the oven better than three Hours, and when it comes out, fkim off the fat, ftrain the Gravy over the beef, and garnifh with pickles.

Bubble   "When 'midft the frying pan,
and   in accents favage,
Squeak. The Beef fo furly, quarrels with
         the Cabbage."

For this as for Hafh, felect those Parts of the joint that have been leaft done ; it

is generally made with ſlices of cold
boiled Salted Beef, Sprinkled with a little
Pepper, and juſt lightly browned with a
bit of Butter in a frying-pan, — if it is
fried too much it will be Hard.

Boil a Cabbage, ſqueeze it quite dry,
and chop it ſmall, take the Beef out of
the Frying pan and lay the Cabbage in
it : Sprinkle a little Pepper and Salt over
it ; Keep the Pan moving over the Fire
for a few minutes. Lay the Cabbage in
midſt of diſh and the meat around it.

Head

Head Cheefe. Boil the fore head, Ears and feet of a frefh Pig until the meat will almoft drop from the Bones, then cut all the meat off in Pieces about three quarters of an inch fquare, Seafon with Pepper, Salt, fage, and fweet marjoram; put thefe pieces into a Stew pan with juft enough of the Liquor in which they were boiled to prevent their Burning; put the ftew pan over a flow Fire, when the pieces are thoroughly heated mix all well together and Pour into a ftrong bag, Prefs the bag between two flat Surfaces, with a fifty pound Weight on top until its contents are quite cold, then Remove the bag and cut the Cheefe into flices.

This is a nice difh at breakfaft.

To make a Scotch Haggafs. Take the Lights, Heart, and Chitterlings of a calf, chop them very fine, and a Pound of Suet chopped fine; feafon with Pepper and Salt to your palate; mix in a Pound of Flour

or Oatmeal, roll it up, and put it in a Calf's Bag and boil it; an Hour and a half will do it.

Some add a Pint of good thick Cream, and put in a little beaten Mace, Cloves, or Nutmeg; or Allfpice is very good in it.

Saufages. Chop fat and lean pork or beef  together, Seafon with fage, pepper, falt, allfpice and nutmeg. Add to this a fourth part of Bread-crumbs foaked in water. Stuff this into well cleaned Hog's-guts. When dreffed obferve to prick them with a Fork.

Gammon of Bacon. Take off the fkin or rind, and lay in Loo-water for two or three hours: Then put it in a Pan, pour over a quart of Canary-wine, let foak half an Hour. When you have fpitted it, put a clean Paper over the fat fide, pour the Canary in which it was foaked into the dripping-pan, and Bafte the meat while it

is

is roafting. When it is enough Dredge it well with crumbled bread and parfley, fhred fine. Make the fire Brifk and brown it well. If you ferve it hot Garnifh with rafpings of bread, but if cold for fecond courfe Garnifh with green parfley.

To Boil a Ham in Syder or Otherwife. This is an Important article, and requires Particular attention in order to render it elegant and Grateful. It fhould be boiled in a large Quantity of Water, or if you prefer it Syder. One quarter of an hour to each Pound. The rind taken off when Warm. It is moft Palatable when cold, and fhould be fent to table with Eggs, horfe-radifh or muftard. This affords a fweet Repaft.

Baked Ham in Cider. Put a pint of Cider and a cup of brown fugar into enough Water to cover the Ham. Boil

three

three hours, or until the Skin will peel off eafily. Remove the Skin, cover the ham with a cruft of fugar and bake in a flow oven, three hours. Diffolve a cup of fugar in a pint of Cider, and bafte frequently while baking.

If the cider is very Sweet ufe lefs fugar.

A Chine of Pork. Make a ftuffing of the fat Half of pork, parfley, thyme, fage, eggs, crumbs of bread ; Seafon it with pepper, falt, fhalot, and Nutmeg, and ftuff it thick : then roaft it gently, and when it is about a quarter Roafted, cut the fkin in flips ; and make your Sauce with apples, lemon peel, two or three cloves, and a Blade of mace : fweeten it, put fome butter in, and muftard in a cup.

To Barbacue a Shoat. Prepare a Pig, about ten weeks old, as for roafting. Make a Forcemeat of two anchovies, fix fage leaves, and the liver of the Pig ; all chopped very Small ; then put them into a mortar with the Crumb of half a penny loaf, four Ounces of butter, half a tea-

44   fpoonful

fpoonful chyan pepper, and Half a pint of red wine. Beat them all Together to a pafte, put it into the Pig's belly and few it up. Lay your Pig down at a good Diftance before a large brifk Fire, finge it well, put into your Dripping-pan three bottles of red Wine, and bafte it well with this all the time it is roafting. When it is half done, put under the Pig two penny loaves, and if you find your Wine too much reduced, add More. When your pig is near enough, take the loaves and Sauce out of your dripping-pan, and put to the fauce one anchovy chopped Small, a bundle of fweet herbs, and half a Lemon. Boil it a few minutes, then draw your pig, put a fmall lemon or Apple in the pig's mouth, and a loaf on each fide. Strain your Sauce, and pour it on boiling Hot. Send it up whole to Table, and garnifh with Barberries and fliced lemon.

To

To make a Brown Friccasey of Rabbits. Take a Rabbit, cut the Legs in three Pieces, and the Remainder of the Rabbit the same Bignefs, beat them Thin, and fry them in Butter over a quick Fire; when they are fried put them in a Stew-pan with a little Gravy, a Spoonful of Catchup, and a little Nutmeg, then fhake it up with a little Flour and Butter, Garnifh your Difh with crifp Parfley.

Jugged Hare. Cut your Hare into fmall pieces, and lard them here and there with little flips of Bacon, feafon them with pepper and falt, and put them in an earthen Jug, with a blade or two of Mace, an onion ftuck with cloves, and a bunch of fweet Herbs. Cover the jug clofe, that nothing may get in; fet it in a pot of boiling Water, and three Hours will do it. Then turn it into the Difh, take out the onion and fweet Herbs and fend it hot to Table.

A fine Way to pot a Tongue, a Fowl and a Goose.

Take a dried Tongue, boil it until it is Tender, then peel it : take a large Fowl, bone it ; a Goose, bone it, take a quarter of an ounce of

Cloves, a large Nutmeg, a quarter of an ounce of black Pepper, beat all together ; a spoonful of Salt ; rub the inside of the Fowl well, put in the tongue; and then season the goose, and fill it with the Tongue and Fowl, and the Goose will look as though it was Whole, lay it in a Pan that will just Hold it and cover with melted Butter, bake it an hour and a half ; then Drain it from the

butter, lay on it a coarse Cloth to cool, put your goose in the Pot and pour butter

47

butter over fo it is an inch above the Meat. It will keep a great While, looks Beautiful and eats fine. When you cut it, it muft be cut Crofsways clear through, and looks very Pretty ; it makes a pretty corner Difh. If you will be at the Expence a Turkey can go outfide of the Goofe.

Pig's Harflet. Wafh and dry fome Liver, Sweetbreads and fat and lean Pieces of Pork, beating the latter with Rolling-pin to make it tender; feafon with Pepper, Salt, Sage, and a little Onion fhred fine ; when mixed, put all into a Crawl and faften up tight with Needle and Thread. Roaft it on a Hanging Jack, or by a String. Serve with a Sauce of Port Wine, Water, and Muftard juft boiled up.

Entrée of Larks. Take eighteen fine *Larks*, pick and bone them, feafon with Salt and Pepper, and ftuff them with Farce fine. Put them into a Difh with fome of the Farce between them, and ornament

the

the Birds with fried Bread cut in fanciful Shapes. In arranging the Birds around the Diſh if any remain raiſe them in the middle above the Reſt: cover with Bacon and bake twenty Minutes. Serve with a rich Sauce.

A Salma- Waſh and cut open at the
gundi. Breaſt two large Dutch or Lochfine pickled herrings; take the meat from the Bones without breaking the Skin, and keep on the head, tails, fins, &c. Mince the Fiſh with the breaſt of a cold roaſt Chicken ſkinned, a couple of hard-boiled Eggs, an Onion, a boned Anchovy, and a little grated Ham or Tongue. Seaſon with ſalad oil, vinegar, cayenne, and ſalt, and fill up the Herring-ſkins, ſo that they may look plump and well-ſhaped. Garniſh with ſcraped horſeradiſh, and ſerve Muſtard with the diſh. — Obſervation. An ornamental Salmagundi was another of the frippery diſhes

of former times. This Edifice was raifed on a china Bowl reverfed, and placed in the middle of a Difh, crowned with what, by the courtefy of the Kitchen, was called a Pine-apple, made of frefh Butter, around were laid, ftratum above ftratum, chopped Eggs, minced Herring and Veal, rafped Meat, and minced Parfley ; the whole furmounted by a triumphal arch of Herring-bone, and adorned with a garnifhing of Barberries and Samphire.

Veal Olives. Take two pounds of Veal, fome Marrow, two anchovies, the yolks of two hard Eggs, a few Mufh-rooms, fome Oyfters, a little bit of thime, marjoram, parfley, fpinage, lemon-peel, falt, pepper, nutmeg, and mace, finely beaten, take your Veal caul, lay a layer of Bacon, and a layer of the Ingredients, roll it in the Veal caul, and either Roaft it or bake it. An hour will do either. When enough, cut in Slices and lay on a Difh with lemon.

OF BREAD, BUNNS AND BREAKFAST CAKES.

Yeaſt. Thoſe who make their own Bread ſhould make their Yeaſt too. One handful of Hops, with two or three handfuls of malt and rye bran, ſhould be Boiled fifteen or twenty minutes in two quarts of Water, then ſtrained, hang on to Boil again, and thicken with half a pint of Rye and water ſtirred up quite Thick, and a little Molaſſes; boil it a minute  or two, and then take it off to Cool. When juſt about Lukewarm, put in a cupful of good lively Yeaſt, and ſet in a cool Place in ſummer, and a warm place in Winter. If it is too Warm when you put in the old yeaſt, all the Spirit will be killed.

Bread. Put twenty-four pounds of Flour into the wooden Bread trough. Make a deep round Hole in the middle

of the Flour, and pour into it diluted
Yeaſt; ſtir into enough of the ſurround-
ing meal as will make it like paſte.
Cover the Mixture with dry flour. Cover
the Mixture well to the depth of at leaſt
an eighth of an inch, and then throw over
the Trough a Cloth.

After ſome time Cracks will appear in
the covering of Flour, when theſe ceaſe
it is Time to make up the Dough. Add
gradually twelve pints of Warm water

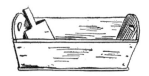

until the whole be-
comes Sufficiently
moiſt to be formed
by Kneading into a
compaċt Maſs. Then Duſt it over with
flour and leave it to Swell. In cold
weather it ſhould be near the Fire. The
maſs is likely to be Diſtended in an
hour if the ferment be good. Then it
may be formed into Loaves.

Straw-
berry
Bread. Take of the berries, Bray
them in a Mortar, mix them
with meal, and make them into
Strawberry Bread.

To prepare the Oven. A brick Oven is the only one proper for the Baking of bread. If you are so unfortunate as to have one of thofe New-fangled, iron ovens. Do not try to ufe it. Send your Bread to the Bakers. The fire fhould be kindled in the Oven when you make up the Dough. There are various ways of Knowing when the Oven is at the right heat. Sprinkle flour on the bottom, and if it burns quickly it is *too hot.* If you cannot hold your hand in to count twenty moderately it is hot enough. When ready Clear out the Afhes and wafh the Bottom of oven with a wet Mop. Put in your loaves with a Bread peel, and if the fire has been well Managed it will bake in one Hour.

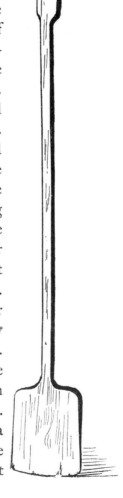

To

To make Bifquit Bread. Take one half a pound of very fine Wheat flour, and as much Sugar finely fcarced, and dry them very well before the Fire, dry the flour more than the Sugar ; then take four new-laid Eggs ; take out the Strain, then fwing them very well, then put the Sugar in, and fwing it well with the Eggs, then put the Flour in, and beat it all together half an Hour at the leaft ; put in fome Anife-feed, or carraway feed, and rub the Plates with butter, and fet them into the Oven.

Apple Bread. Mix ftewed and ftrained Apple, or grated apple uncooked, with an equal quantity of Wheat flour ; add Yeaft enough to raife it, and mix Sugar enough with the apple to make it quite Sweet. Make it in Loaves, and bake it an hour and a half, like other Bread.

Pilgrim Cake. Rub two Spoonfuls of Butter into a Quart of Flour, and wet it to Dough with cold Water. Rake open a Place in the hotteſt part of the Hearth, roll out the Dough into a Cake an Inch thick, flour it well on both Sides and lay it on the hot Aſhes, cover it with hot Aſhes and then with Coals. When cooked wipe off the Aſhes and it will be ſweet and good.

Hom-
miny
Bread. Their Bread alſo they make of the Homminy ſo boiled, and mix their Flower with it, caſt it into a deep Baſon in which they form the Loaf, and then turn it out upon the Peel, and preſently put it into the Oven before it ſpreads abroad : the Flower makes excellent Puddins.

Indian
Corn
Biſcuits. To one-half pound of Butter, add ſix ounces pounded Sugar, and three Eggs well beaten ; when well Mixed, add three-quarters of a pound of Cornflower, a little Nutmeg, and ſome Caraway ſeeds ; beat well, and bake on little Tins.

Waffles.

Waffles. To a quart of Milk add five Eggs, one and one quarter pounds of Flour, one half pound of Butter; beat them well Together; when baked fift Sugar and cinnamon on them. If you make the Waffles before it is time to Bake them, add a fpoonful of Yeaft.

Beaten Bifquit. Warm one tablefpoonful of Lard or butter in equal quantities of Milk and water, as much as will make a quart of Flour a very Stiff dough. Beat the Dough for thirty Minutes with an Axe or rolling Pin. Work it very Smooth. Roll it Thin and cut it into round Bifquits, and prick full of Holes. About fix minutes will Bake them.

Naples Bifcuit. Take one pound of Sugar, one pound of Flour, ditto of Eggs, beat to a Froth, put the fugar in by
56 Handfuls,

Handfuls, beat it very Well, then add the Flour in the fame Manner, carraway feed and as much rofe water as agreeable.

Johnny Cake or Hoe Cake. Scald one pint of Milk and put two thirds Indian meal and one third Flour, add falt, Molaffes, and fhortening, Work up with cold water pretty Stiff, and bake before the Fire.

Indian Slap-Jack. One quart of Milk, one pint Indian Meal, four Eggs, four fpoons Flour, a little Salt, beat together. Baked on Gridles, or fry in a dry Pan or baked in a pan which has been rubbed with fuet. Spat them down with a fpoon. This makes a nice Mefs for breakfaft with Maple fyrup.

Pink Pancakes. Pancakes of a beautiful pink colour are eafily made by the following fimple Procefs. Boil till tender a large Blood-beet root, bruife it in a marble Mortar. Put to it the Yolks

of

of four Eggs — two Spoonfuls of Flour, three of Cream, half a grated Nutmeg, Sugar to palate and a Glafs of Brandy ; mix them well together, fry them carefully and ferve them up with a garnifh of Sweet meats.

Pan-Cakes. Pan-Cakes fhould be made with half a pint of Milk, falt, three great fpoonsful of Sugar, fpiced with Cinnamon, Cloves, Rofe-water or Lemonbrandy, juft as you happen to have it. Flour ftirred to make a batter. If you have no Eggs or wifh to fave them fupply the Place of eggs with two or three fpoonsful of Lively emptings, but they muft ftand five or fix hours to Rife. A fpoonful or more of New England Rum makes pan-cakes Light. Flip makes very nice Pan-cakes. In this cafe nothing is done but to Sweeten your mug of beer with Molaffes : put in one glafs of N. E. rum, heat it till it Foams by putting in a red hot Poker : and ftir it up with Flour as thick as other Pancakes.

58   *Tops*

Tops and Bottoms. Beat the Yolks of eight Eggs and the whites of Four with a quarter of a pint of Yeaſt. Melt a quarter of a pound of Butter in half a pint of new Milk warm from the Cow. Strain it into a pound and a half of flour with two ounces of Beaten ſugar. Make it up into a Batter and ſet before the Fire for half an Hour. Then work up into a little more Flour. Bake in tins two inches ſquare in Breadth and three inches High, flattened on all Sides. When baked let them ſtand to Cool, then part them in two and  brown a Little. If made about like a Sauce, and eaten after the firſt Baking, they are very nice buttered for Tea.

French Ruſks. Weigh a pound of Yolks of eggs and a pound and a half of beaten Sugar. Stir them well about for ten Minutes. Add an ounce of caraway-ſeed and two pounds of Flour. Mix to-gether in a paſte and Mould upon a clean

Pye-

Pye-board into rolls fourteen or fifteen inches long, and between two or three inches Thick. Lay thefe on a paper, and Prefs them with the Hand till about an inch in thicknefs, and to a point at the Edges. Put them on a wire Plate, with two or three papers under. Bake with care, and Wet the paper to take it off. Cut with a fharp Knife into rufks about a quarter of an inch thick. Put in the Oven till crifp and Dry.

Bunns. At Night take three cups of Milk, one cup of fugar, one cup of good Lightening. Thicken with Flour as thick  as Pan-cakes. Let rife til Daylight; then add one cup of fine fugar, one cup of fweet Butter, two fmall fpoonsful of pearlafh, with pleafant fpices. Mix the whole ftif as Bifquit. Leaf it again till very Light, then roll out your Bunns, place them on Tins. Leaf them a fhort Time, and bake quickly. Then thou wilt have bunns which, with butter to prevent Adhefion to

60   thy

thy Mouth, eat as thou mayeſt have
Appetite.

Sally This Cake is called after the
Lunn. Inventreſs. Sift into a pan a
pound and a half of Flour. Make a hole
in the middle, and put in two ounces of
Butter warmed in a Pint of Milk, a ſalt-
ſpoonful of Salt, three well beaten Eggs,
and two table-ſpoonfuls of the beſt freſh
Yeaſt. Mix the flour well into the other
ingredients, and put into a ſquare tin
Pan that has been greaſed with Butter.
Cover it, ſet it in a Warm place, and
when it is Light, bake it in a moderate
Oven. Send to table hot and eat with
Butter. Or, you may bake it in Muffin-
rings on a griddle.

Muffins. Lay a quarter of a pint of Ale
yeaſt of as light a Colour as can be got,
into cold water for over Night. The
Next Morning pour the Water off clear
from it. Put a quart of loo-Water into
it, with a quarter of an ounce of Salt, let
ſtand five or ſix Minutes. Strain this

into

into half a peck of fine Flour. Mix it lightly and let it lie in the Trough for an hour to rife, covered with Flannel. Pull the dough into fmall pieces, roll them thin with a Rolling-pin well floured, lay them directly under a flannel, and they will rife to a proper Thicknefs. Bake them upon a hot Hearth. When done on one fide turn on the other, but they muft not be Browned. They eat very Well.

Crumpets. The Dough may be made as for the Muffins. When it has ftood to rife give it a Roll with the hands, pull it into little Pieces about the fize of a Small pul- 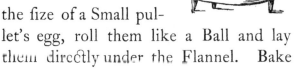 let's egg, roll them like a Ball and lay them directly under the Flannel. Bake on a hot Hearth lightly brown.

Turtu-longs fine for Break-faft. Take a quarter of a pound of Butter, three ounces of powdered Sugar, one pound and a half of Flour, fix eggs yolks and whites Together, and a very little falt, and mix them Altogether on

your

your Dreffer, and have a preferving Pan on the fire, with Clean boiling water in it, roll your batter out about four inches Long and almoft as Thick as your little finger. Join it in two round Rings, the two ends of them, and put them into this boiling Water, not too many at a Time: then on the other fide, have a Bafon with cold water, and as the Bifquits fwim on the top of the boiling Water, take them out, put them in the Cold water, and let them lie all Night: take them out the next Morning, put them in a fieve, and Drain all the water fiom them: put them on your plate without any paper under, let your Oven be very hot, and Watch them, and you will fee them Rife very much, the more the Better. See they are not burnt, but let them be of a fine Brown, then take them out, and Serve them up.

Short Cake. If you have Sour-milk or Butter-milk you better make Short-cake for Tea. Rub a bit of fhortening or three tablefpoons of Cream with the Flour: put a teafpoonful of ftrong dif-

folved

folved Pearlaſh into your four milk, mix rather Stiff and bake in a Spider on a few Embers.

Tea Cakes. Dry a pound and a half of Flour before the fire. Beat up the Yelks of two eggs with two ſpoonsful of good Lightning. Add three quarters of a pint of new Milk. Strain through a Sieve into the flour. Mix into a Dough and let ſtand before the Fire an hour. Make up into cakes like

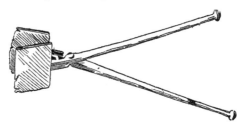

a Saucer. Let ſtand alittle, then half an hour will bake them. Spread with Butter when pulled open and ſerve.

Wafers. Two tableſpoonfuls of rolled white Sugar, two Tableſpoonfuls of But-

ter

ter, one Coffee-cup of Flour, and eſſence
of Lemon or Roſe-water to flavor. Add
Milk enough for a thick Batter, Bake
in Wafer Irons buttered, and ſtrew on
white Sugar.

———

Of Milk, Butter, Cheese and Eggs.

To Make Butter. As ſoon as you have Milked,
Strain your Milk into a Pot and
ſtir it often for Half an Hour,
then put it away in your
Pots or Trays. When it's
Creamed, ſkim it exceed-
ingly Clean from the Milk,
and put your Cream into
an Earthen Pot, and if you
do not Churn immediately
for Butter, ſhift your Cream
once in twelve Hours into
another clean Pot.

When you have Churned,
Waſh your Butter in three
or four Waters, and then Salt it as you
will have it, and Beat it well. Let it

5   65   ſtand

ſtand in a Wedge if it be to pot, till the next Morning, beat it again and make your Layers the thickneſs of three Fingers, and then ſtrew a little Salt on it. And ſo do until your Pot is full.

To take Rancid Taſte from Butter. When freſh Butter has not been Salted in proper Time, or when Salt Butter has become Rancid or Muſty, after melting and ſimmering it, dip in it a Cruſt of Bread well Toaſted on both Sides, and in a few Minutes the Butter will loſe its diſagreeable Taſte.

To make Fairy Butter. Take the Yolks of two hard Eggs and beat them in a Mortar with a large Spoonful of Orange-flower Water, and two Teaſpoonsful  of fine Sugar beat to Powder ; beat this all to a fine Paſte, then mix with as much freſh Butter out of the Churn, and force it through a fine Strainer full of Holes into a Plate. This

is

is a pretty Thing to fet off a Table at Supper.

To Roaſt a pound of Butter. Lay it in Salt and Water two or three Hours, then fpit it and rub it all over with Crumbs of Bread, with a little grated Nutmeg, lay it on the fire, and as it roafts bafte it with the Yolks of two Eggs and then with Crumbs of Bread all the Time it is roafting ; but have ready a Pint of Oyfters ftewed in their own Liquor, and lay in the Difh under the Butter. When the Bread has foaked up all the Butter, brown the Outfide, and lay it on your Oyfters. Your fire muft be very flow.

To prepare Rennet. Take the Stomach of a young Calf, and having taken out the Curd contained therein, wafh it clean and falt it thoroughly infide and out, leaving a white Coat of Salt over every Part of it. Put it into an earthen Jar and let it ftand three or four Days. Take it out

of

of the Jar and hang it up to drain two or three Days. Re-falt it, plunge it again in a Jar; cover it tight down with a Paper pierced full of Holes by a large Pin, and in this State it ought to remain twelve Months. It may be uſed, however, a few Days after the ſecond ſalting; but it will not be ſo Strong as if kept a longer Time.

Sage Cheeſe. Take the tops of young red Sage, and having preſſed the Juice from them by beating in a Mortar,  do the ſame with the Leaves of Spinach, and then mix the two Juices together. After putting the Rennet to the Milk, pour in ſome of this Juice, regulating the Quantity by the Degree of Colour and Taſte it is intended to give to the Cheeſe. As the Curd appears break it gently, and in an equal Manner; then emptying it into the Cheeſe-Vat, let it be a little Preſſed in order to make it eat Mellow.

Having

Having ſtood for about ſeven Hours, Salt and turn it daily for four or five Weeks, when it will be fit to Eat.

To make a Brick- Bat Cheeſe. Take two Gallons of new Milk and a Quart of good Cream, heat the Cream, put in two Spoonsful of Ren- net, and when it is come, breaк it a little, then put it into a wooden Mold in the Shape of a Brick. It muſt be half a Year old before you eat it ; you muſt preſs it a little, and ſo dry it.

Cream Cheeſe. The Conſiſtency of Cream increaſes by Expoſure to the Air. In three or four Days it becomes ſo thick that the Veſſel which contains it may be inverted without its being Spilt. In eight or ten Days it becomes a ſoft Solid, and its ſurface becomes tough. It has now no longer the Flavour of Cream, but has acquired that of Cheeſe. This is the Proceſs for making what is termed Cream Cheeſe.

Welſh

Welſh Galli-maufry. Mix well in a Mortar, Cheeſe with Butter, Muſtard, Wine, flavoured Vinegar, or any Ingredients admired, *ad libitum.*

Welſh Rabbit.
" Happy the man that has each fortune tried,
To whom ſhe much has given and much denied,
With abſtinence all delicates he ſees
And can regale himſelf on Toaſt and Cheeſe."

Cut a Slice of Bread about half an Inch thick, pare off the Cruſt and Toaſt it very ſlightly on both Sides, ſo as juſt to brown it without making it Hard or burning it. Cut a Slice of Cheeſe (good fat mellow Cheſhire Cheeſe is the beſt) a quarter of an Inch thick, not ſo big as the Bread by half an Inch ; pare off the

Rind,

Rind, cut out all the Specks and rotten Parts (rotten Cheefe toafted is the *ne plus ultra* of Haut Goût, and only eatable by the thoroughbred Gourmand in the moft inverted State of his jaded Appetite), and lay it on the Toafted Bread in a Cheefe Toafter, carefully watch it that it does not burn, and ftir it with a Spoon to prevent a Pellicle forming on the Surface. Have ready good Muftard, Pepper, and Salt. If you obferve the Directions here given, the Cheefe will eat mellow and will be uniformly done, and the Bread crifp and foft, and will deferve its ancient appellative of a " Rare Bit."

Obs. Ceremony feldom triumphs more completely over Comfort than in the ferving out of this Difh ; which to be prefented to the Palate in perfection, it is imperatively indifpenfable that it be introduced to the Mouth as foon as it appears on the Table.

Another Welfh Rabbit. Toafted Bread buttered on both Sides profufely, then a Layer of cold Roaft Beef, with Muftard

Muftard and Horfe-Radifh. Then a
Superftratum of Chefhire Cheefe thor-

oughly faturated
while toafting with
cw*rw*, or if abfent
genuine Porter, Black
Pepper and Efchalot-Vinegar.

Obfer- Eggs keep very well when
vations you can exclude Air, which is
on Eggs. beft done by placing a Grate in
any running Water, and putting Eggs as
the Hens lay them on the upper Side,
then let them lie till you want to ufe
them, when they will be as if laid that
Day. In Places where they may be
ftolen, make a Cheft with Holes for the
Water to Pafs through.

N. B. The Water muft continually
cover the Eggs. Mill-dams are proper
Places.

A Boil fix Eggs hard, peel them
pretty and cut them in thin Slices.
Difh of Put a quarter of a Pound of
Eggs. Butter in a Stew Pan, then put
in your Eggs and fry them quick. Then

lay

lay them in a Difh before the Fire. Pour out all the Fat, fhake in a little Flour, and two Shalots cut fmall; throw them into the Pan, pour in a quarter of a Pint of White Wine, a little Juice of Lemon and a Piece of Butter rolled 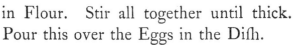 in Flour. Stir all together until thick. Pour this over the Eggs in the Difh.

Egg and Bacon Pie. Steep a few thin Slices of Bacon all Night in Water to take out the Salt, lay your Bacon in the Difh, beat eight Eggs with a Pint of thick Cream, put in a little Pepper and Salt and pour it on the Bacon, lay over it a good cold Pafte, bake it in a moderate Oven. Very good eaten cold.

Poached Eggs. The Cook who wifhes to difplay her Skill in poaching muft endeavour to procure Eggs that have been laid a couple of Days. Thofe that are

new

new laid are too milky. The Beauty of a poached Egg is for the Yolk to be feen blufhing through the White, which fhould only be juft fufficiently hardened to form a Tranfparent Veil for the Egg. This is done by carefully flipping the Egg into boiling Water until the White fets.

Mar-malade of Eggs, the Jews' Way. Take the Yolks of twenty-four Eggs, beat them for an Hour; clarify one Pound of the beft moift Sugar, four Spoonfuls of Orange Flower Water, one Ounce of blanched and pounded Almonds; ftir all together over a very flow charcoal Fire, keeping ftirring it all the while one Way till it comes to a Con-fiftence; then put it into Coffee Cups, and throw a little beaten Cinnamon on the Top of the Cups.

Eggs on Toaft. Having cut Toaft, brown it, lay it on your Difh, butter it, and very carefully break fix or eight Eggs on the Toaft. Take a red hot

74   Shovel

Shovel and hold it over them. When they be done, fqueeze a Seville Orange

over them, grate a little Nutmeg over it and ferve it up.

Amu-lets. Take fix Eggs, beat them up as fine as you can, ftrain them through a hair Sieve, and put them into a frying Pan, in which muft be a quarter of a Pound of hot Butter. Throw in a little Ham fcraped fine, with fhred Parfley, and feafon them with Pepper, Salt and Nutmeg. Fry it brown on the under Side, and lay it on your Difh, but do not turn it. Hold a hot Salamander over it for half a minute, to take off the raw Look of the Eggs. Stick curled Parfley in it, and ferve it up.

Two Truths concern-ing Eggs. *Roafted Eggs* are incomparably better than boiled.

Never eat any Butter with Eggs in the Shell. You cannot imagine how much more you will have of

their

their Flavour and how much Eaſier they will ſit upon your Stomach.

To fry Eggs as Round as Balls. Having a deep frying Pan and three Pints of Clarified Butter heat as hot as for Fritters, and Stir it with a Stick till it runs round like a Whirlpool. Then break your Egg in the Mid-

dle and turn it round with your Stick till it be as hard as a poached Egg ; the whirling around of the Butter will make it like a Ball. Then take it up with a Slice and ſet it in a Diſh before the Fire. So you may do as Many as you pleaſe.

OF THE KITCHEN GARDEN.

To dreſs Roots and Greens. Always be very careful that your Greens be nicely picked. Boil them in a Copper or Saucepan. Uſe no Iron Pans for they

are

are not proper; but let them be copper, brafs, or Silver. Moft people fpoil garden things by overdoing. All things that are Green fhould have a little Crifpnefs or they have neither Sweetnefs nor Beauty. If your Water is hard, put in a fmall Spoonful of Salt of Wormwood previous to laying in your Vegetables.

Sampe — Take the Indian
A kind of Wheat beat in a
Loblolly. Mortar and Sift
the Flower out of it: the
Remainder called Homminey Put into a Pot of
two or three Gallons with
Water, and boyl it upon a
gentle Fire till it be like
Hafty Puddin: they put of this into Milk and to eat it.

Hull One Quart of Indian Corn,
Corn. one Gallon of Water, one Quart of ftrong Lye, boil until the Hulls come off, Wafh it in Cold Water, then boil till Tender and eat in Milk.

Succotafh

Succotafh. One Pint of Beans and one Pint of Corn, half a Pound of Pork or Bacon, a Pint of Water and a Pint of Milk. Cook about four Hours.

Soyer Potato. Take a large Potato and cut out a round Piece as big as a Shilling through the Potato; put in the Scoup and take out fome of the Infide, fill this with Saufage Meat or Veal. Cover the Hole with Part of what you cut out and Bake with cut Part utmoft.

Potato-Snow. Choofe White, Mealy, Smooth Potatoes; Skin them, boil them carefully, and when they crack pour off

the Water, and put them to dry on the Trivet till quite dry and powdery. Rub them through a coarfe wire-Sieve on the Difh they are to go to the table on; and do not move it or the Flakes will Fall and Flatten.

A Potato Collar. A Potato - Collar, rolled handfomely up, fcored in diagonal Lines, and nicely Browned, makes a good Potato-Difh. Garnifh it with Potato Balls around it, and a Brown Onion Gravy-Sauce, or plain melted Butter, which we would recommend in place of the Wine Sauce ordered by learned Cooks.

To fry Parfnips to look like Trout. Take middling Sort of Parfnips, not too thick, boil them as for eating : peel and cut them in two the long way. Only ufe the fmall Ends, beat three or four Eggs, put to them a Spoonful of Flour, dip in your Parfnips and fry them in Butter a Light Brown. Ufe for Sauce a little Butter and Vinegar, and fo Serve them up.

Squafhes

Squashes A pleasant Food Boyled and
or Squon- Buttered and Seasoned with
ter- Spice. The Apple-Squash is
Squashes. the best Kind.

Skirrits. The sweetest, whitest and most
pleasant of Roots. Wash them thoroughly Clean and when you have boyled
them until tender, Skin the Roots and
Cut them in Slices. Have ready a little
Cream, Piece of Butter rolled in Flour,
Yelk of an Egg, Nutmeg, some White
Wine, Stir all together, and when enough,
pour over the Roots.

Cabbage Take one Pound of Beef Suet
Pudding. and as much of the Lean part
of a Leg of Veal. Then take a little
Cabbage well washed and scald it. Bruise
the Suet, Veal, and Cabbage together in
a marble Mortar and season it with
Mace, Nutmeg, Ginger, a little Pepper
and Salt, and put in some Green Goose-
berries, Grapes, or Barberries. Mix them
all well with the Yolks of four or five Eggs
well beaten. Wrap all up together in a

green

green Cabbage Leaf, and tie in a Cloth. It will take about an Hour to boil.

Kidney Beans. Put fome young and fmall Beans into a ftrong Salt and Water for three Days, Stirring them two or three Times each Day. Then put them into a Pan with Vine Leaves both under and over them, and pour on them the fame Water they came out of. Cover them Clofe and fet them over a very flow Fire till they be of a very fine Green. Then put them into a hair Sieve to Drain, and make a Pickle for them of White Wine Vinegar or fine Ale Allegar. Boil it five or fix Minutes with a little Mace, Jamaica Pepper, long Pepper, and a Race or two of Ginger Sliced. Then pour it Hot upon the Beans, and tie them down with a Bladder and Paper.

Cale-Cannon. Boil feparately fome Potatoes and Cabbage. When done, Drain and Squeeze the Cabbage, and

Chop or Mince it very Fine. Mafh the Potatoes and Mix them gradually but thoroughly with the Chopped Cabbage, adding Butter, Pepper and Salt. There fhould be twice as much Potatoe as Cabbage.

Cale-cannon is eaten with Corned Beef boiled Pork or Bacon.

Arti- Wring the Stalks off and lay
chokes. the Artichokes in Water cold with the Bottoms up ; by which means the Dirt concealed between the Leaves will boil out. After the Water boils, they will take nearly two hours to be done. Serve with melted Butter, Salt and Pepper.

Sallets. Leaves eaten raw are termed Sallet Herbs, they Correct the prutruf- cent Tendency of Animal Food. They make a pleafant Addition to other Ali- ments and have a graceful Look on the Dinner Table. Lettuce is the princi- pal Ingredient in thefe vegetable Meffes, altho' the blanched Foot Stalks of the

Celery

Celery or Smallage is liked by fome for its nutty Flavour. A Variety of other Herbs mingle in full well felected Sallets fuch as Sorrel, Endive, young Onions, Cucumbers, Succory, Crefs, Radifh, Leaflets, etc. Many mild Herbs are ufed as Salading. As the Compofure of Sallet is quite a dainty and jaunty Branch of the Culinary Art we would recommend that young Ladies in the Country gather their own Sallet Herbs and drefs the Sallets for their Families as in the Hurry of the Stewpan and the Spit the Dinner Hour is too diftracting for the Cook to do juftice to fo gallant a Difh.

Foreigners call many things Sallets. We would merely mention cold little dreffed Difhes. Sallets are likewife compounded of Cold Oyfters, Salmon, Cray-Fifh, etc., but thefe Gothic Mixtures are feldom or never touched.

The Spanifh fay that it requires four Perfons to make a good Sallet. A

Spendthrift

Spendthrift for Oil, a Mifer for Vinegar, a Counfellor for Salt and a Madman to ftir it up.

Slow. For Cold Slow nothing more is neceffary than to cut a Cabbage into fmall ftrips and leave it lie in Cold Water for half an Hour. It fhould be cut in the fame manner for hot Slow, leaving out the ftalky Part. Melt in a Pot a Piece of Butter the Size of a Hen's Egg or fome nice Top Pot, put in the Cabbage, ftir till Tender, add Salt and Pepper and a Cup of Vinegar.

Hops. They are to be boiled in Water with a little Salt and eat as a Salad with Salt, Pepper, Oil, and Vinegar.

To drefs Cucum- bers. Pare and flice the Cucumbers thin, and with a Pen-knife cut the Slices into fmall Skeins (the Length of the Difh) wound up. Drefs thefe along the Difh, and pour Vinegar over. Cucumbers thus cut may be Served over Beet-root fliced. Cucumbers in Skeins may alfo be ferved Cooked.

A Salad and Salad Sauce. Let the Herbs be frefh-gathered, nicely Trimmed and Picked and Wafhed in Salt and Water, drain and cut them. Juft before Dinner rub the Yolks of two hard boiled Eggs very Smooth on a Soup-plate with a very little rich Cream. When well mixed add a Teafpoonful of made Muftard, a little Salt, a Spoonful of Olive-Oil, one of oiled Butter and when this is Mixed put in as much Vinegar as will give the proper Degree of Mellifluence —about two large Spoonful: Add a lit-  tle pounded Lump Sugar if the Flavour is liked. Put this Sauce in the Difh and lay the Cut Herbs lightly over it; or mix them well with it, and garnifh with Beet-root Sliced and marked, Rings of the Whites of Eggs in Chains young Radifhes, etc. Salads admit of many elegant Decorations of contrafted Colour as fcraped Horferadifh, fquirted Fairy Butter, Plovers and Sea-Birds Eggs.

N. B. Some knowing Perfons like

grated

grated Parmefan put to their Salad and
Sauce.

All Sorts of Pastry.

" Unlefs some Sweetmeat at the bottom
     lye
Who cares for all the Crinkling of a
     Pye?"

A Lum-   Take a pound and a half of
ber Pye.   a fillet of Veal and Mince it
with the fame quantity of Beef fuet.
Seafon it with fweet fpice, Five Peppers,
and a handful of fpinage and a Head of
Lettuce, Thyme, and Parfley. Mix it
with a penny grated white Loaf, the
Yolk of an Egg, fack, and Orange-
flower Water, a pound and a half of
Currants. Humble Pye is made the
fame way.

A Lear   Take Claret, Gravy, Oyfter-
for Sav-   Liquor two or three Anchovies
oury   a Faggot of Sweet Herbs and
Pyes.   an Onion; boil it up and
        thicken

thicken with Brown Butter, then pour into your Savoury Pies when called for.

A Caw-dle for Sweet Pyes Take Sack and White Wine alike in quantity, a little Verjuice and Sugar, boil it and brew it with two or three Eggs, as butter'd ale; when the Pyes are baked, Pour it in at the Funnel and ſhake it together.

Beef Stake Pie. Take Slices of Beef Stake, half an Inch thick lay them three Deep in a Paſte, adding Salt, Pepper and Slices of raw Onion between each laying, duſting Flour at the same Time together with a ſufficient Quantity of Butter. Add half Pint water, bake one and a half Hour. Put in an earthen Veſſel and cover with a Cruſt.

A Foot Pie. Scald Neat's feet, and clean them well (grafs fed are beſt) put them into a large Veſſel of cold

water,

Water, which change daily during a Week, then boil the Feet till Tender.

 Take away the Bones: when cold, chop Fine. Add one Pound Beef Suet, four Pounds Apples raw. Chop together very Fine. Add one Quart of Wine, two Pounds ftoned Raifins, one Ounce Cinnamon one Ounce of Mace. And Sweeten to your Tafte. Bake in a Pafte three quarters of an Hour.

A Sea Pie. Four Pounds Flour, one and a half of Butter rolled in a Pafte wet with cold Water. Line the Pot therewith. Lay in fplit Pigeons one Dozen with Slices of Pork, Salt, Pepper, and duft on Flour doing thus till the Pot is full, or your Ingredients expended. Add three Pints of Water. Cover Tight with Pafte, and ftew Moderately two and half Hours.

Marrow Pafties. Make your little Pafties the Length of your Finger, and as

broad

broad as two Fingers, put in large Pieces of Marrow, dipped in Eggs, and feafoned with Sugar, Mace, Nutmegs; Stew a few Currants over the Marrow. Bake or fry them.

To Make Pafties to Fry. Take the Kidney of a Loin of Veal or Lamb, Fat and all, fhred it very Small; feafon it with a little Salt, Cloves, Mace, Nutmegs, all beaten Small, some Sugar and the Yolks of three hard Eggs minced fine. Mix all thefe together with a little Sack or Milk or Cream. Put them in Puff pafte and fry them. Serve them Hot.

Oyfter Patties. Put a fine Puff-cruft into small Patty Pans, and cover with Pafte, with a bit of Bread in each; and againft they are Baked, have ready the following, to fill with, taking out the Bread.

Take off the Beards of Oyfters, cut

the

the other Parts into fmall Bits; put them into a fmall Toffer with a Grate of Nutmeg, the leaft White Pepper, and Salt; a Morfel of Lemon Peel, cut fo fmall you can fcarcely See it, a little Cream and a little of the Oyfter Liquor. Simmer a few Minutes before you fill.

Obferve to put a Bit of Cruft in all Patties to keep them Hollow while baking.

Fried Apple Pies. Make a fweet Cruft, roll and cut out with a Saucer. Fill with Apple Sauce, double over the Crufts and pinch the Edges. Fry in fmoking Fat. To be eaten hot for Supper.

Cherry Pie. Cherry Pies fhould be baked in a deep Plate. Take the Cherries from the Stalks, lay them in a

Plate,

Plate, and fprinkle a little Sugar, and Cinnamon, according to the Sweetnefs of the Cherries. Bake with a Top and bottom Cruft three quarters of an Hour.

Whortle- Whortleberries make a very
berry good common Pie, where there
Pie. is a large Family of Children.
Sprinkle a little Sugar and fifted Cloves on each Pie. Bake with a Cruft.

Cuftard It is a general Rule to put
Pie. eight Eggs to a Quart of Milk
in making Cuftard Pies; but fix Eggs are plenty for any Common Ufe. The Milk should be Boiled and Cooled before it is ufed; and Bits of Stick-cinnamon and Bits of Lemon-peel boiled in it. Sweeten to your Palate with clean Sugar; a very little Sprinkling of Salt makes them Better. Grate in a Nutmeg. Bake in a deep Plate. About twenty Minutes are

ufually

ufually Enough. If you are Doubtful whether they are Done, dip in the Handle of a Silver Spoon, or the Blade of a fmall Knife; if it comes out Clean, the Pie is done. Do not pour them into your Plates till the Minute you put it in the Oven, it makes the Cruft Wet and Heavy. To be baked with an Under Cruft only. Some People bake the Under Cruft before the Cuftard is poured to keep it from being Clammy.

To make Sweet-meat Tart. Make a little Shell Pafte, roll it, and line your Tins, prick them in the Infide, and fo bake them; then you may Serve them up in any Sort of Sweet-meats, what you pleafe. You may have a different Sort every Day, do but keep your Shells by you.

To make Kick-fhaws. Make Puff Pafte, roll it thin, and if you have any Moulds, work it upon them; make them up with Preferved Pippins;

you

you may Fill fome with Goofeberries, fome with Rafpberries, or what you pleafe ; then Clofe them up, and either fry or bake them ; throw grated Sugar over them and Serve them up.

Goofe-berry Tart. Lay clean Berries and fift over them Sugar, then Berries and Sugar, till a deep Difh be filled intermingling a Handful of Raifins and one Gill of Water. Cover with the following Pafte.

Rub half a Pound of Butter into one Pound of Flour, four Whites beat to a Foam, two Ounces of fine Sugar.

Bake fomewhat longer than other Tarts.

To Make Fine Cheefe-cakes. Take a Pint of Cream, warm it and put it to five Quarts of Milk warm from the Cow, then put Rennet to it, and give it a Stir about : and when it is come, put the Curd in a linen Bag, and let it draw well away from the

Whey

Whey but do not Squeeze over much: then put it in a Mortar, and break the Curd as fine as Butter: put to your Curd half a Pound of Sweet Almonds blanched and beat exceeding Fine, and half a Pound of Mackeroons beat alfo: then add to it the Yolks of nine Eggs beaten, a whole Nutmeg grated, two perfumed Plums diffolved in Rofe or Orange Flower Water, half a Pound of fine Sugar. Mix all well together, then melt a Pound and a quarter of Butter and ftir it well in it, and half a Pound

 of Currants plumped, to let ftand to cool till you ufe it: Then make your Puff Pafte thus: take a Pound of fine Flour, wet it with cold Water, roll it out, put into it by Degrees a Pound of frefh Butter, and fhake a little Flour over each Coat as you roll it. Make it juft as you ufe it.

N. B. You may leave out the Currants, for Change; nor need you put in the perfumed Plums, and for Variety

when

when you make them of Mackeroons
put in as much Tincture of Saffron as
will give them a high Colour, but no
Currants: this we call Saffron Cheefe
cakes, the other without Currants
Almond Cheefe cakes: with Currants
fine Cheefe cakes: with Mackeroons,
Mackeroon Cheefe cakes. Do not put
them into the Coffins until juft as they
go into the Oven.

Boiled One Cup boiled Cider; one
Cider Cup Flour; two Cups Water;
Pie. two Cups Molaffes; mix thoroughly with two Crufts. This will
make enough for feveral Pies.

An Herb Pick two Handfuls of Parfley
Pie. from the Stems, half the
Quantity of Spinach, two Lettuces,
fome Muftard and Crefs, a few Leaves of
Forage and White-beet leaves. Wafh
and Boil them a little. Cut fmall, lay
in a Difh with fome Salt. Mix a Batter
with Flour, two Eggs, a Pint of Cream,
pour over. Cover with a Cruft and bake.

Squab

Squab Pie. Cut Apples as for other Pies and lay them in Rows with Mutton Chops. Shred Onion and Sprinkle it among them alfo fome Sugar.

Pour over them about a Pint of Water and Cover with a good Pafte.

Pumpkin Pie. Take out the Seeds and pare the Pumpkin; Stew and Strain it through a Colander. Take two Quarts of fcalded Milk and eight Eggs and ftir your Pumpkin into it; fweeten it with Sugar or Molaffes to your Tafte. Salt this Batter and feafon with Ginger, Cinnamon, or grated Lemon Peel to your Mind. Bake with a Bottom Cruft.

Mince Pies excellent. Take about a Pound of very tender Beef, two Pounds of Suet and about two Pounds of Currants; Cloves and Mace to your Tafte; Lemon Peel and the Juice of

two

two good Lemons, White Wine and Red
fufficient to moiften the Meat. Add
fome Sweetmeats (if you Pleafe) beat
the Spice with a little Salt and fweeten
with moift Sugar to your Tafte. Bake for
one Hour between two Layers of Pafte.

*To make
an Apple
Pie.*   Make a good Cruft and lay
it around the Sides of a deep
Difh, pare, quarter and take
out the Cores of your Apples.

Lay a Row of Apples thick, then
fome Sugar, throw over a little Lemon-
peel minced fine, fqueeze a little Lemon,
then a few Cloves,
then the reft of your
Apples and more
Sugar. You muft
fweeten to your Pal-
ate, and fqueeze a little more Lemon.

Then boil in fair Water the Peelings
and Cores with a Blade of Mace till it
is very good; then Strain it and Boil it
with Sugar till there is but very Little
and Good. Pour this into your Pie.
Put on a Cruft and Bake it.

If you Pleafe you may put in a little Quince or Marmalade.

OF PUDDINGS.

Obferva- In boiled Puddings take a
tions on Care that the Cloth be very
Pud- Clean not Soapy but dipped in
dings. hot Water and Floured. If a
Bread Pudding, tie it Loofe, if a Batter,
tie Clofe. Be fure that the Water boils.
Puddings fhould be Served with the firft
Courfe.

Minute One Quart of fweet Milk
Pudding. boiling, and three Eggs. Beat
the Flour and Eggs well together and
ftir it all in your Milk until Thick
enough for Pudding. This eats well
with Sugar and Cream.

Hafty Boil one or two Quarts of
Pudding. Water according to your Family, fift your Meal and wet fome of it
with Cold Water and pour in Salt to

your

your Liking, then ftand over the Kettle and Sprinkle in Meal Handful after Handful and beat like Mad with the Pudding Stick letting it boil between Whiles. When it is Labourious to ftir it, it is enough. It takes at leaft half an Hour. Eat with Milk or Treacle.

Either Indian or Rye Meal may be ufed. If the Syftem is in a re-ftricted State nothing can be better than Rye Hafty Pudding and Weft India Molaffes. This Diet would fave Many a one from the Horrors of Dyfpepfia.

To make Take a Quart of Ready-boiled *Furmity.* Wheat, two Quarts of Milk, a quarter of a Pound of Currants clean Picked and Wafhed; ftir them Together and boil them; beat up the Yolks of three or four Eggs, a little Nutmeg, with two or three Spoonfuls of Milk, and add to the Wheat; ftir them together for a few Minutes; then fweeten to your Palate, and fend it to Table.

To

To make a Flummery Caudle. Take a Pint of fine Oatmeal and put it to two Quarts of fair Water. Let it ftand all Night, in the Morning ftir it and ftrain it into a Skillet with three or four blades of Mace and Nutmeg quartered, fet it on the Fire and keep it ftirring and let it boil a quarter of an Hour, if it is too Thick put in more Water and let it boil Longer; then add a Pint of Wine, three Spoonfuls of Orange Flower Water, the

Juice of two Lemons and one Orange, a bit of Butter and as much Sugar as will Sweeten it. Let all thefe have a Warm, and thicken it with the Yolks of two or three Eggs.

Drink it hot for Breakfaft. When Cold it eats very pretty with Cyder and Sugar.

Baked Goofe-berry Pudding. Stew the Goofeberries in a Jar over a hot Hearth till they Pulp. Take a Pint of Juice rubbed through a coarfe Sieve

and

and beaten with the Yolks and Whites of three Eggs, beaten and ſtrained, and one and one half Ounces of Butter. Sweeten it well, and put a Cruſt around the Diſh. A few Crumbs of Roll ſhould be mixed with the Above to give a little Conſiſtence.

Cherry Pudding. For Cherry Dumpling make a Paſte about as rich as you make Shortcake, roll it out, and put in a Pint and a half or a Quart of Cherries, according to the ſize of your Family. Double the Cruſt over the Fruit, tie it up Tight in a Bag and boil one Hour and a half.

A Grate-ful Pudding. To a Pound of Flour add a Pound of White Bread grated. Take eight Eggs, but only half the Whites; beat them up, and mix with them a Pint of new Milk. Then ſtir in the Bread and Flour, a Pound of Raiſins ſtoned, a

Pound

Pound of Currants, half a Pound of Sugar, and a little beaten Ginger. Mix all well together, pour it into your Diſh and ſend it to the Oven. If you can get Cream inſtead of Milk it will be a Material Improvement.

Cranberry Pudding. A Pint of Cranberries ſtirred into a Quart of Batter made like a Batter Pudding is very nice eaten with a Sweet Sauce.

Yorkſhire Pudding. This nice Diſh is uſually baked under Meat, and is thus made : Beat four large spoonsful of Flour, four Eggs and a little Salt for fifteen Minutes. Then put to them three Pints of Milk and Mix them well Together. Then butter a Dripping Pan and ſet it under Beef, Mutton, or Veal while Roaſting. When it is Brown, cut it in ſquare Pieces and turn it over ; and when the under Side is browned alſo, ſend it to Table on a Diſh.

To

To make Black Puddings. First before you kill your Hog get a Peck of Grits, boil them half an Hour in Water, then Drain them and put them into a Clean Tub or large

Pan, then kill your Hog, and fave two Quarts of the Blood of the Hog, and keep Stirring it till the Blood is quite Cold, then mix it with your Grits and ftir them well Together. Seafon with a large Spoonful of Salt a quarter of an Ounce of Cloves, Mace and Nutmeg together, an equal Quantity of each: dry it, beat it well and Mix in. Take a little Winter Savory, Sweet Marjoram and Thyme, Pennyroyal ftripped off the Stalks for a Flavour. The next Day take the Leaf of the Hog cut in Dice, fcrape and wafh the Guts, tie one End and begin to Fill them. Put in much Fat, and when three-quarters Full tie the other End. Prick them with a Pin and boil them an Hour. Take out and lay on clean Straw.

To

To make fry'd Toasts. Chip a Manchet well and cut it round Ways in Toasts, then take Cream and eight Eggs, seasoned with Sack, Sugar and Nutmeg and let these toasts steep in it about an Hour then fry them in Sweet Butter. Serve them up with plain Melted Butter or with Butter, Sack and Sugar. As you please.

To make Apple Fritters. Take four Eggs and beat them very well, put to them four Spoons full of fine Flour, a little Milk, about a Quarter of a Pound of Sugar, a little Nutmeg and Salt, so beat them very well together ; you must not Make them very thin, if you do it 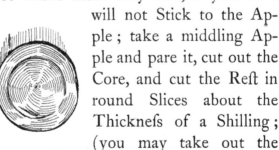 will not Stick to the Apple ; take a middling Apple and pare it, cut out the Core, and cut the Rest in round Slices about the Thickness of a Shilling ; (you may take out the Core after you have cut it with your Thimble) have ready a little Lard in a

Stew-

Stew-pan or any other deep Pan; then take your Apples every Slice fingle, and dip it into your Batter, let your Lard be very hot, fo drop them in, you muft keep them turning till Enough, and mind that they are not too Brown; as you take them out, lay them on a Pewter Difh before the Fire till you have Done; have a little White-Wine, Butter, and Sugar for the Sauce, grate over them a little Loaf Sugar and ferve them up.

To make Apple Dump-lins. Take Half a Dozen Coddlings or any other good Apples, Pare and Core them. Make fome Cold Butter Pafte, and roll it about the Thicknefs of your Finger. So lay around every Apple, and tie them fingle in a fine Cloth, boil them in a little Salt and Water and let the Water boil before you put them in. Half an Hour will boil them. You muft have for Sauce a little White-Wine and Butter. Grate fome Sugar round the Difh and Serve them up.

Oatmeal Dumplin or a Fitlefs Cock. This antique Scotch Dish, which is now feldom feen at any Table, is made of Suet and Oatmeal, with a Seafoning of Pepper, Salt and Onions, as for White Puddings, the Mixture bound together with an Egg, and Moulded fomewhat in the form of a Fowl. It muft be Boiled in a Cloth like a Dumplin.

Tanfey Pudding. This is with many a Favourite in the Spring. Bruife fufficient Tanfey to obtain three Table Spoonfuls of its Juice; pour it on as much Crumb of French Roll as will imbibe it. Pound three Ounces of blanched Almonds to a fine Pafte with two Ounces of Loaf Sugar, the fame Quantity of Butter, and a Tea-Spoonful of grated Seville Orange Peel. Beat up a Pint of Cream with fix Eggs and Mix all the Ingredients thoroughly together. This Pudding may be either boiled or baked; if the Former, it requires a Sauce

of

of melted Butter, Sugar, and Lemon Juice.

To make White Pot. Take two Quarts of new Milk, eight Eggs and half the Whites beat up with a little Rofe-Water, a Nutmeg, a Quarter of a Pound of Sugar — cut a Penny-Loaf in very thin Slices, and pour Milk and Eggs over. Put a little Bit of fweet Butter at the Top. Bake in a buttered Difh for one Hour.

Bread and Butter Pudding. Slice Bread fpread with Butter and lay in a Difh fpread with Currants between each Layer, and Zeft if it be very Nice. Pour over an unboiled Cuftard of Milk two or three Eggs a few Pimentos and a very little Watafia two Hours at leaft before it is to be Baked.

Quaking Pudding. Scald a Quart of Cream, when almoft Cold, put to it four Eggs well beaten, a Spoonful and

half

half of Flour, fome Nutmeg and Sugar,  tie it Clofe in a buttered Cloth and boil an Hour. Turn it out with Care left it fhould Crack.

Hunters Mix a Pound of Suet, ditto *Pudding.* Flour, ditto Currants, ditto Raifins ftoned and a little Cut, the Rind of half a Lemon fhred as fine as Poffible, fix Jamaica Peppers in fine Powder, four Eggs, a Glafs of Brandy, a little Salt, and as little Milk as will make it of a proper Confiftence. Boil it in a floured Cloth or Melon Mould eight or nine Hours. Serve with Sweet Sauce. Add fometimes a Spoonful of Peach Water for a Change.

This Pudding will keep after boiled fix Months if tied up in the fame Cloth and hung up, folded in a Sheet of Cup Paper to preferve it from the Duft. When to be ufed it muft boil a full Hour.

CREAMS,

" Here find they entertainment at the
    Height
In Cream and Coddlings rev'ling with
    Delight."

Goofe-
berry
Fool.
Take a Quart of Goofeberries :
pick, Coddle and bruife them
very well in
a Marble Mortar or
Wooden Bowl, and rub
them with the Back of

a Spoon thro' a Hair-Sieve, till you take
out all the Pulp from the Seeds : take a
Pint of thick Cream, mix it well among
your Pulp, grate in fome Lemon-Peel
and fweeten it to your Tafte. Serve it
either in a China
Difh or an
Earthen one ac-
cording to your
Fancy.

Apple Fool may be made the fame by
pulping the Apples.

For *Orange Fool* beat three Eggs very

109   well,

well, add the Juice of three Seville
Oranges and Cook till like Butter.   Nutmeg and Cinnamon to your Palate.

*To make
a Sylla-
bub from
the Cow.*
Put a Pint of Cider and a
Bottle of ſtrong Beer into a
large Bowl, grate in a Nutmeg,
and ſweeten it to your Palate.
Then Milk from the cow as much milk
as will make a ſtrong Froth.   Let it
ſtand an Hour, and then Strew over it
a few Currants well waſhed, picked, and
plumed before the Fire ; and it will be
Fit for uſe.

*To make
Whipt
Syllabubs.*
Take a Quart of thick Cream
and half a Pint of Sack, the
Juice of two Seville Oranges
or Lemons, half a Pound of double re-
fined Sugar, pour it in a broad earthen
Pan, and whiſk it well : but firſt Sweeten
ſome Red Wine or Sack and fill your
Glaſſes as full as you chooſe then as the
Froth riſes take it off with a Spoon, and
lay it on a Sieve to drain : then lay it
carefully on your Glaſſes till they are as

full

full as they will hold. Do not make thefe Long before you ufe them. Many ufe Cyder fweetened, or any Wine you pleafe or Lemon or Orange Whey made thus. Squeeze the juice of a Lemon or Orange into a quarter of a Pint of Milk. When the Curd is hard pour the Whey clear off and Sweeten to your Pal-ate. You may Colour fome with the Juice of Spinach, fome with Saffron and fome with Cochineal (juft as you Fancy).

To make Take a Quart of thick Cream
Whipt and the Whites of eight Eggs,
Cream. beat well with half a Pint of
Sack : mix it together and Sweeten to your Palate with double refined Sugar. You may Perfume it (if you pleafe) with a little Mufk or Ambergris tied in a Rag and Steeped a little in the Cream. Whip it up with a Whifk and fome Lemon Peel tied on the Whifk. Lay the Froth on your Glaffes or Bafins or over a fine Tart.

Chrift-

Chrift-
mas
Bowl.

Break nine Sponge Cakes half a Pound of Mackaroons in a deep Difh : pour over one Pint Raifin Wine, half Pint Sherry, leave them to foak, Sweeten with two Ounces of Powdered Sugar Candy and pour over one Pint and a half of Cuftard. Stick with two Ounces Sliced Almonds Place on a Stand and Ornament with Chriftmas Evergreens.

A Froth
to fet on
Cream
Cuftard
or Trifle
which
looks and
eats well.

Sweeten half a Pound of the Pulp of Damfons or any Sort of Scalded Fruit, put to it the Whites of four Eggs beaten, and beat the Pulp with them until lt will Stand as High as you Choofe, and being put on the Cream with a Spoon will take any Form. It fhould be Rough to imitate a Rock.

Almond

Almond Beat the Almonds fine with
Cuſtards. Roſewater in a Mortar. Beat
four Yelks of Eggs with two Spoonsful
of Sugar. Whiſk a Pint of Cream until
it is Light. Mix all together and pour
in Cups.

The You may take a Soup-Diſh
Floating according to the Size and Quan-
Iſland. tity you would Make, but a
A pretty Pretty Glaſs Diſh is beſt, and
Diſh for ſet it on a China Diſh ; firſt
the Mid- take a Quart of the thickeſt
dle of a Cream you can get, make it
Table. pretty Sweet with fine Sugar, pour in
a Gill of Sack, grate the yellow Rind o
a Lemon in, and mill
the Cream till it is all
of a thick Froth ; then
carefully pour the Thin
from the Froth into a
Diſh ; take a French
Roll, cut it as Thin as
you can, lay a Layer

of that as Light as poſſible on the Cream,
then a Layer of Currant Jelly, then

French Roll, and then Hartſhorn Jelly, then French Roll, and over that whip your Froth that you have Saved off the Cream very well Milled up, and lay at Top as High as you can Heap it ; and as for the Rim of the Diſh, ſet it Around with Fruit or Sweet Meats according to your Fancy. This looks very pretty in the Middle of a Table with Candles around it, and you may make it as many Colors as you happen to have Jams or Sweetmeats, but that is as you Fancy.

To Make a Bieſt Cuſtard. Take a Pint of Bieſt, ſet it over the Fire with a little Cinnamon, or three Bay Leaves, let it be boiling Hot, then take it Off, and

have ready Mixed one Spoonful of thick Cream ; pour your hot Bieſt upon it by Degrees, mix it exceeding Well together, and Sweeten it to your Taſte ; you may either put it in Cruſts or Cups to Bake it.

To make
White
Leach.
Take half a Pound of Almonds Blanch and beat them with Rofe Water and a little Milk ; then ftrain it Out, and put in a Piece of Ifing-glafs, and let it boil on a Chafing-Difh of Coals half an Hour ; then Strain it in a Bafon and Sweeten it, and put a Grain of Mufk in it, and let it Boil a little longer, and put to it three or four Drops of Oil of Mace or Cinnamon and keep it till it's Cold.

To make
Blomonge.
Take one Pint of Milk and half a Handful of picked Ifinglafs, put the Ifinglafs into the Milk and boil it, till all the Ifinglafs is Melted ; Strain it through a Sieve ; pound four ounces of Sweet, and fix or feven Bitter Almonds very Fine ; put a little Spice in your Milk, when you Boil it, mix your Almonds with the Milk to make it Palatable : pafs it through a Sieve again, put it in your Moulds, and let it Stand till it is Cold.

Waffail-

Waſſail-Bowl, a centre Supper Diſh. Crumble down as for Trifle a nice freſh Cake (or uſe Macaroons or other ſmall Biſcuit) into a china Punch-Bowl or deep Glaſs Diſh. Over this pour ſome ſweet rich Wine, as Malmſey Madeira, if wanted very Rich, but Raiſin-Wine will do. Sweeten this, and pour a well-ſeaſoned rich Cuſtard over it. Strew Nutmeg and grated Sugar over it, and ſtick it over with ſliced blanched Almonds. This is, in fact, juſt a rich eating Poſſet.

A very good Waſſail-Bowl may be made of Mild-Ale well ſpiced and ſweetened, and a plain Rice-Cuſtard made with few Eggs. The Waſſail-Bowl was anciently Crowned with Garlands and Ribbons.

Curds and Cream. Put four Quarts of new Milk to warm and add a Pint to a Quart of Buttermilk according to its Sourneſs. Cover until the Curd is of Firmneſs to cut three or four Times

acroſs

acrofs with a Saucer, as the Whey leaves
it. Lade it into a Shape and fill it till it
be Solid enough to take the Form.
Serve with a Whip of Cream, Sugar,
Wine and Lemon.

Rennet   If   your   Hufband   brings
Pudding. Home   Company   when   you
have not made Ready, Rennet Pudding
can be made at
Five   Minutes
Notice   provided
you keep a Piece of Calf's Rennet ready
Prepared, Soaking in a Bottle of Wine.
One Glafs of this wine with Sugar and
Nutmeg to your Tafte will Make a pleaf-
ant Cold Cuftard.

Clouted   String four Blades of Mace on
Cream. a Thread, put them in a Gill of
new Milk and fix Spoonfuls of Rofe-
water, fimmer a few Minutes, then by
Degrees ftir this Liquor ftrained into the
Yolks of two new Eggs well beaten. Stir
the Whole into a Quart of very good
Cream, and fet it over the Fire. Stir it till

Hot,

Hot, but not Boiling Hot, pour it in a deep Difh, and let Stand twenty-four Hours. Serve it in a Cream difh to eat with Fruits. Many prefer it without any Flavor but the Cream ; in that Cafe ufe a Quart of new Milk and the Cream. When it is Enough, a round Mark will appear on the Surface of the Cream the Size of the Bottom of the Pan it is done in. This they call the Ring, and when feen Remove from the Fire.

Curd *Puffs.* Put a little Rennet into two Quarts of Milk, and when it is Broken, put it into a coarfe Cloth to drain. Then rub the Curd through a Hair Sieve and put it in four Ounces of Butter, ten Ounces of Bread, half a Nutmeg, a Lemon Peel grated, a Spoonful of Wine. Sweeten with Sugar to your Tafte, rub your Cups with Butter and put them in the Oven for about half an Hour.

A Trifle. Fill a Difh with Bifcuit finely broken, Rufk and Spiced Cake, wet with

Wine, then pour a good boiled Cuftard (not too Thick), over the Rufk, and put a Syllabub over that ; garnifh with Jelly and Flowers.

A Standing-Difh in New England. Put into a Pottle of Milk about ten or twelve Spoonf-ful of Silper beaten Small in a Morter. So Boyle it leifurely, Stirring of it every Foot leaft it burn too ; when it is almoft boiled Enough, they hang the Kettle up higher, and let it Stew only, in fhort Time it will Thicken like a Cuf-tard ; they Seafon it with a little Sugar and Spice, and fo Serve it to the Table in deep Bafons, and it is altogether as Good as a White Pot.

To make Steeple Cream. Take five Ounces of Hartf-horn and two Ounces of Ivory, and put them in a Stone Bottle, fill it up with fair Water to the Neck, put in a fmall Quantity of Gum-Arabic, and Gum-Dragon, then tie up the Bottle very

119   Clofe,

Clofe, and fet it into a Pot of Water, with Hay at the Bottom : let it ftand fix Hours, then take it out and let it Stand an Hour before you Open it, left it fly in your Face ; then Strain it out, and it will be a ftrong Jelly ; then take a Pound of blanched Almonds, beat them very Fine, mix it with a Pint of rich Cream, and let it Stand a Little. Then mix it with a Pound of Jelly, fet it over the Fire till it is fcalding Hot, fweeten to your Palate with double-refined Sugar, then take it Off, put in a little Amber, and pour it into fmall high Gallipots, like a Sugar-Loaf at Top. Turn them out, and lay around them Heaps of whipt Cream.

Devonſhire Milk the Cow into a Bowl
Junket. in which a little Rennet is
put. Stir it up when

Full ; and when Firm pour over it fcalded Cream, pounded Sugar, and Cinnamon.

For Cod-   Codle forty fair Codlings,
ling Cream. green and tender, then Peel
them and Core them, and Beat them,
Strain them with a Quart of Cream and
Mix them well Together in a Diſh, with
fine Sugar, ſack and Roſe Water.

A Hedge-   Take two Pounds of blanched
Hog.   Almonds, and beat them well
in a Mortar, with a little Canary and
Orange-Flower Water to keep them from
Oiling. Work them into a ſtiff Paſte,
and then beat in the Yolks of twelve, and
the Whites of ſeven Eggs. Put to it a
Pint of Cream, ſweeten it to your Taſte,
and ſet it over a clear Fire. Keep it con-
ſtantly Stirring till it is Thick enough to
make in the Form of an Hedge-Hog.
Then Stick it full of blanched Almonds,
ſplit and ſtuck up like the Briſtles of a
Hedge-Hog, and then put it into a Diſh.
Take a Pint of Cream, and the Yolks of
four Eggs beat up, and ſweeten it to your
Palate. Stir the Whole over a flow Fire
till it is quite Hot, and then pour it into
the Diſh round the Hedge-Hog, let it
Stand

Stand till it is Cold, when it Forms a pleafing Effect.

Of All Sorts of Cakes.

Obfer-vation on Cake. It was a Miftake of old to think that the White of eggs made cakes and puddings heavy ; on the Contrary, if beaten long and Separately they contribute greatly to give Lightnefs.

Indepen-dence Cake. Twenty pounds of flour, fifteen pounds of Sugar, ten Pounds of butter, four dozen eggs, one quart of Wine, one quart of brandy, one Ounce of nutmeg, cinnamon, cloves, currants, raifins, five pounds Each, one quart of yeaft. When Baked froft with Loaf fugar ; drefs with box and gold Leaf.

Queens Cake. Whip half a pound of Butter to a cream, add one pound of fugar, ten eggs, one Glafs of wine, half a

gill

gill of Rofe water and fpices to your Tafte. All worked into one and one quarter pounds of flour. Bake in a Quick oven in about Ten Minutes.

Pound Cake. Take One pound of Sugar, one pound of butter, one pound of flour, ten eggs, one gill rofe water, fpices to your Tafte ; Watch it well, it will bake in a Slow oven in about Fifteen minutes.

Old Hartford Election Cake. Five pounds of Dried and Sifted flour, two pounds of butter, two pounds of fugar, three gills of Diftillery Yeaft, or twice the quantity of Home Brewed, four eggs. A gill of Wine and a gill of Brandy. Half an ounce of nutmegs, Two pounds of Fruit, One quart of Milk.

Rub the Butter into the Flour, then add the Yeaft, then Half the milk, hot in winter, blood warm in Summer, then the eggs Well beaten, the Wine and the Remainder of the Milk.

Beat

Beat it well, and let it ſtand to riſe over Night. Beat it Again in the morning, adding the brandy, the ſugar, and ſpice. Let it riſe three or four hours, till very Light. When you put the Wood into the oven put the Cake into buttered Pans, and put in the Fruit as directed previouſly.

If you wiſh it richer add a pound of Citron.

Great Grand-mother Cole's Fried Cakes. Take ſome Cream in a Bowl, break in an egg or two and ſome Sweetning, then put in one Thing and another til its juſt right. Have your Lard het hot, and if you uſe your Judgment they 'll be good.

Shrewſ-bury Cakes. Take to one Pound of Sugar, three Pounds of Fineſt Flour, a nutmeg Grated, ſome beaten Cinamon; the Sugar and Spice Muſt be ſifted into the Flour, and Wet it with

Three

Three Eggs and as much melted Butter as will Make it of a good Thickneſs to roll into a Paſte ; Mould it well and Roll it, cut it into what Shape you pleaſe. Perfume Them, and prick them before they go into the Oven.

Molly Starke's Fruit Cake. ("'Tis victory to-night my boys, or Molly Starke's a widow.")
Three Cups of Sugar, five Cups of Flour, one Cup of Butter, one Cup of four Cream, five Eggs, one Glaſs of Wine, one pound of Raiſins, one Teaſpoon Pearlaſh, Spices at your Pleaſure.

To make Jumbals. Take the whites of three Eggs, beat them Well, and take off the Froth ; then take a little Milk, and a little Flour, near a pound, as much Sugar ſifted and a few Carraway-ſeeds Beaten very fine ; work all theſe together into a stiff Paſte, and make them into what Form you Pleaſe. Bake them on white paper.

To

To make Wiggs. Take four pounds of Flower, half a pound of fugar, one nutmeg Grated, a Little falt, and one ounce of Carraway feed, then mix them with Your Flower, with one ounce of Coriander feed well Bruifed, then fet over the Fire, a pint of Milk with a pound of butter, till the butter be juft Melted, then put in your flower, a pint of Yeft and four eggs not Beaten, mix all into a

pafte but not ftiff, then role them into wiggs and put them on tinn Plates and Bake them in a quick Oven. Lay them on paper as you Drain them, and fo eat them when you are Hungry.

General Training Cake. One bowl of Milk, one bowl butter, one bowl of yeaft, two and one half bowls of fugar, two and one half bowls of raifins, four bowls of flour, three eggs.

Chop one half of the Raifins, Cinnamon and Cloves.

Dutch

Dutch Pudding, or Albany Cake. Mix two pounds or Rather lefs of good flour with a pound of butter, Melted in half a pint of milk. Add to This the whites and Yolks of eight eggs Separately well beaten, a half-pound of fine Sifted fugar, a pound of cleaned Currants, and a few chopped almonds or a little Candied orange-peel fliced fine. Put to this four Spoonfuls of Yeaft. Cover it up for an Hour or two, and bake it for an hour in a Wide flattifh difh. When cold it Eats well as a Cake.

Cyder Cake. Cyder cake is very good to Bake in fmall loaves. One pound and a half of Flour, half a pound of butter, half a pint of cyder, one Teafpoonful of Pearlafh ; fpice to your Liking. Bake till it Turns eafily in your Pans. I fhould think about half an Hour.

Federal Cake. Take one half a Pound of flour, fix ounces of Butter, the Same of fugar, one egg, beat Well. Add rofe water and Spice.

127   *Ballance*

Ballance Ballance twelve eggs with fugar,
Cake. add one
half the weight of
flour, and a Little
mace.

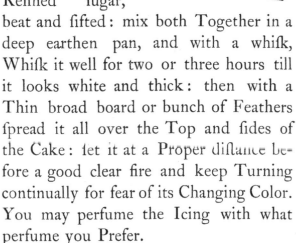

To ice T a k e
a great the whites
Cake. of twenty-
four Eggs and a
pound of double-
Refined fugar,
beat and fifted: mix both Together in a
deep earthen pan, and with a whifk,
Whifk it well for two or three hours till
it looks white and thick: then with a
Thin broad board or bunch of Feathers
fpread it all over the Top and fides of
the Cake: fet it at a Proper diftance before a good clear fire and keep Turning
continually for fear of its Changing Color.
You may perfume the Icing with what
perfume you Prefer.

Whiftles. Half a pound white fugar,
Quarter of a pound of butter, and fix
eggs,

eggs, the Whites and yelks beaten Separately. Stir the fugar and butter to a Cream, then add the eggs Previoufly beaten, and fifted flour to Make a Thick Batter: flavor with rofewater, if you like. Drop the Mixture by the large fpoonful onto buttered paper. The mixture fhould be Dropped feveral inches Apart, and Spread out Thin. Bake then till of a light Brown, on a board, which will not be over five Minutes. Lay them on a Moulding-board that has white fugar Sprinkled on it; roll them on a ftick while Warm. When cold fill them with any kind of Jelly that is Thick.

Old Connecticut Receipe for Ginger-Cake.   I always take fome Flour: juft enough Flour for the Cakes I want to make: I mix it up with fome Butter-milk, if I happen to have it, juft enough for the Flour, then I take fome Ginger; fome like more, fome like lefs: I put in a little Salt and Pearlafh, and then I tell John to pour in Molaffes till I tell him to ftop.

Plumb-Cake. Take fix pounds of Currants, Five pounds of Flour, an ounce of Cloves and Mace, a little Cinnamon, blanched Almonds, half a pound of Sugar, three quarters of a Pound of Sliced Citron, Lemon and Orange peel, half a pint of fack, a little Honey water and a quart ot Ale yeaft, a quart of Cream, a Pound and a half of Butter melted and poured into the middle thereof; then ftrew a little Flour thereon and let it lie to rife, then work it Well together and lay it before the fire to rife, then Work it up till it is Very fmooth, then put it in a Hoop with a Paper floured at the Bottom.

Crullers. Two pounds of flour; one pound of butter; one pound of fugar; fix eggs; and one Nutmeg, grated; mix them well together, roll half an inch thick, and cut them in fancy Shapes,

or

or make them in rings, and drop them in
Boiling lard.

To make You muſt take four pounds of
a rich the fineſt Flour, and three
Seed pounds of double-refined Sugar
Cake beaten and fifted ; Mix them to-
called
Nun's gether, and dry them
Cake. by the Fire till you
prepare the other Materials ;
take four pounds of Butter,
beat it with your Hand till it
is ſoft like cream ; then beat
thirty-five eggs, leave out Sixteen whites,
ſtrain off your Eggs from the tread, and
beat them and the Butter together till all
appears like butter ; put in four or five
Spoonfuls of roſe or orange flower water,
and beat again ; then take your Flour
and ſugar, with fix ounces of carraway-
feeds, and Strew them in by Degrees,
and beating it up all the Time for two
hours together ; you may put in as much
tinčture of Cinnamon, or Ambergris as
you pleaſe ; butter your Hoop, let it
ſtand three hours in a Moderate oven.

You muft obferve always, in beating of butter to do it with a cool Hand, and beat it always one Way.

To make Ginger-bread Cake. Take three pounds of flour, one pound of fugar, one pound of butter, rubbed in very Fine, two ounces of ginger beat fine, a large nutmeg Grated ; then take a pound of Treacle, a quarter of a pint of cream, make them Warm together, and make up the bread Stiff; roll it out, and make it up into thin Cakes, cut them out with a fmall glafs, or roll them round like nuts, and bake them on tin Plates, in a flack Oven.

To make Ginger-bread Mrs. Prat's way. Take fix pounds of Flower, two ounces of Ginger, two ounces of caraway feed, half a Pound of powdered loafe fugar. Mix thefe well Together, neet it with four pounds of clarified Treakle, mix it till there is no Flower to be feen, then take a

pound

pound of butter and work it in for fome
Time.   Make it in what Fafhion you
pleafe.

Confects for Routs and Balls.

To make   Take three pounds of Flour
Little   finely dried, three ounces of
Crack-   Lemon and Orange Peel dried
nels.   and beaten to powder, one ounce
of Coriander feeds beaten fine and fearced ;
Mix thefe together with fifteen eggs, half
the whites taken out, a quarter of a pint
of Rofewater, as much Orange   Flower
Water. Beat the
Eggs and Water
well together ;
then put in your
Orange   Peel
and Coriander-
feeds and beat
very well with two fpoons, one in each
Hand ; then beat your fugar in little by
little, then your Flour by a little at a
time, fo beat with both Spoons an Hour

longer, then ftrew Sugar on Papers, and drop them the Bignefs of a Walnut and fet them in an oven. The Oven muft be hotter than when your Pyes are drawn. Do not touch them with your finger before they are Baked. Let the Oven be ready for them againft they are done. Be Careful that the Oven does not Colour them.

To make March-pane. Take a pound of Jordan Almonds blanch and beat them in a mortar, then put to them three quarters of a Pound of double-refined Sugar, and beat with them a few Drops of Orange-flower water; beat all together till 't is a very good Pafte; then roll it into what fhape you pleafe; To ice it

 fcarce double refined Sugar as fine as Flour, wet it with Rofe-water, and with a Feather fpread it over your March-pane. Bake them in an oven that is not too Hot.

Rout-   Mix two pounds of Flour,
Drop   one ditto of Butter, one ditto of
Cakes.   Sugar, one ditto of Currants,
clean and Dry, then wet into a ſtiff Paſte
with two eggs, a large ſpoon of Orange-
flower, ditto Roſe-
water, ditto ſweet
wine, ditto brandy, drop them in a tin
Plate floured : A very ſhort Time bakes
them.

Cocoa-   One pound of grated Cocoa-
nut   nut, only the white part. One
Drops.   pound ſifted white Sugar. The
whites of ſix Eggs, cut to a ſtiff Froth.
You muſt have enough Whites of eggs
to wet the whole Stiff. Drop on buttered plates the ſize of a Penny and bake
immediately.

Milk   Take a quarter
fruit   of a pound of
Biſcuits. Preſerved orange
peel and cut it in Pieces
about half an inch long
and not quite a quarter

     Wide :

Wide: then take fix ounces of Angel-
ico, cut it the fame Way as the orange
peel; put fome whites of egg, Sugar and
orange flower water in a Bafon, and
make an iceing: then put all thefe into
it and paper your Plate three papers,
make them what Size you chufe, then
take a little brufh and Touch them here
and there with a little Cochineal color:
let your Oven be moderately Hot juft
to dry the iceing, as it will Stick together well: let them be Cold, and they
will be like a piece of Rock, &c.

Ratafia Bifquit. Take half a pound of bitter
Almonds and half a pound of
Sweet almonds, and pound them in a

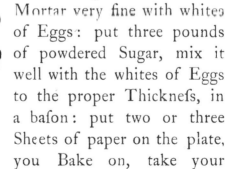

Mortar very fine with whites
of Eggs: put three pounds
of powdered Sugar, mix it
well with the whites of Eggs
to the proper Thicknefs, in
a bafon: put two or three
Sheets of paper on the plate,
you Bake on, take your
Knife and the Spaddle, made of wood,

and drop them on the Paper: let them be round and about the fize of a Nutmeg: put them in the Oven, which muft be Quick, let them have a fine Brown and all alike: let them be Cold before you take them off the Paper.

Frefh Barberry Bifcuits. Take your Barberries, and put them in the Oven: pafs them through a Sieve, and allow to every two pounds of Barberries, five pounds of powdered Sugar fifted through a lawn Sieve: mix the Sugar with the Barberries: break four Eggs, put the whites in a copper pan, and Whifk them very ftrong, mixing them with the Jam: glaze fome thick white Paper, cut it in fmall Pieces, and make them in fmall fquare Boxes, commonly called Coffins: put the jam in as fmooth as poffible, and put them in a fieve: then put them in your Oven, and let them be in fix or eight Days. When dry tear the paper off and put them in your Papered box.

Orange Take China oranges, and peel
Praw- the Rind off in four quarters;
longs. take all the White off from the
infide of the Rind; cut the yellow rind
in pieces about one inch long,
and about the tenth part of
an inch Wide; have a pan of
boiling Syrup on the fire,
and let it boil till it comes
almoft to Caramel; put the
Prawlongs in, and ftir them
with a large wooden fpoon till they are
cold; then put them in a large fieve,
and Shake them, juft to let the fugar that
does not Stick to them go through the
fieve; Put them in your box and keep
them in a dry Place.

Burnt Take fine Jordan almonds
Almonds and fift all the Duft from them;
White. then have fome Syrup boiling
in a pan, and let it Boil till it comes almoft to caramel; put your almonds in
and ftir till they are Cold; pick them
in your fieve, break thofe that Stick together, and then have another pan of
138   Syrup

Syrup boiling, the fame as before, and give them two coats of Sugar; when done, Pick them from each other.

Piftachio Prawlongs are made in a fimilar manner.

To candy **Take it in April, boil it in**
Angelica. Water until tender, then drain it from the water very Well, then fcrape the outfide of it and Dry it in a clean Cloth and lay it in a Syrup, and let it lie in three or four Days and cover it clofe. The Syrup muft be ftrong of fugar, and keep it Hot a good while, and let it not Boil; after it is heated  a good While lay it upon a pie plate and fo let it Dry, keep it near the fire left it Diffolve.

Candied **This is Prepared in nearly**
Eringo. the fame way as Candied Angelica, but the Roots are only flit and Wafhed three or four times in Cold water before they are put into the Syrup.

Little

Little Steep gum tragacanth in Rofe-
Devices water, and with fome double
in refined Sugar make it up into a
Sugar. Pafte. You may colour your
Powders and jellies as your Fancy fhall
direct you, and then make them up into
what Shape you like. You may have
Moulds made into what fhape you
Pleafe, and they will be pretty Orna-
ments placed on the tops of iced Cakes.

 In the middle of
them put little pieces
of Paper, with fome
pretty fmart Scn-
tences written on them, and they will
Afford much mirth to the younger part
of a Company.

To make Take half a gill of Sack, half
Peepper a quarter of an ounce of whole
Cakes. white Pepper, put it in, and Boil
it together a quarter of an Hour; then
take the pepper out, and put in as much
double-refined Sugar as will make it like
a pafte; then drop it in what fhape you
Pleafe on plates, and let it Dry itfelf.

Ginger Tablet. Melt a pound of loaf Sugar with a little melted Butter over the Fire, and put in an ounce of powdered Ginger: keep it Stirring until it begins to rife into a Froth, then pour it into pewter Plates to cool; the platter muſt be rubbed with a little Oil, and then put them in a china Diſh and ſend them to Table. Garniſh with flowers of any Kind.

Sugar of Roſes in Various Figures. Chip off the white Part of ſome Roſe buds and dry them in the Sun: bray an ounce of them in a Mortar, then take a pound of loaf-Sugar, wet it with Roſe - water and boil to a Candy height: then put in your powder of  Roſes and the juice of a lemon. Mix well Together, and then put it on a flat Diſh, and cut it into lozenges, or any kind of Shape your fancy may draw. You may gild or color them to your Taſte.

141   *Barley*

Barley Sugar. Take a fmall Stew pan, put fome fyrup into it, and boil it till it comes to a Caramel: rub a little butter on a marble Stone juft to Greafe it that it may not ftick: then take your fauce-pan by the Handle and let the fyrup run out of the Spout along the ftone in long fticks: twift it while Hot at each end.

To Candy any fort of Flowers. Take the beft treble-refined fugar, break it into Lumps, and dip it piece by piece into Water, put them in a veffel of filver, and melt them over the Fire:  when it juft Boils ftrain it and fet it over the Fire again, and let it boil till it draws Hairs: then put in the Flowers and fet them in glaffes: when it is of a hard candy, Break it in lumps and lay it as High as you pleafe. Dry in the fun.

Candied Take an ounce of race *Ginger.* Ginger grated fine, a pound of loaf Sugar beat fine, and put them into a Preferving-pan, with as much water as will diffolve the fugar. Stir them well Together over a very flow Fire till the fugar begins to Boil. Then ftir in another pound of Sugar, beat fine, and keep Stirring it till it grows thick. Then take it off the fire, and Drop it in cakes upon earthen Difhes. Set them in a Warm place to dry, and they will be Hard and brittle, and look White.

PRESERVES, CONSERVES, AND SYRUPS.

To Pre-ferve Cher-ries in Brandy. Cut the Stalks half off, put them in a Jar, and fill them up with Brandy fweet-ened to your tafte with Sugar-candy, pour in a little currant Jelly, diffolved at the Top, and tie them down for Ufe.

143   *Apple*

Apple Take new Cider preffed from
Butter fweet Apples, and boil down
or Cider from four to one. Then pare
Apple and core fweet Apples, and put
Sauce into the fyrup and Cook until
tender. Skim out and put in More. If
the Weather is warm it may be neceffary
to Reduce the whole Batch.

Black Take any kind of Ripe ber-
Butter. ries, and put to them half their
weight of brown Sugar. Bruife and
feethe them Gently for half an hour, ftirring them Frequently. This is an Elegant fubftitute for butter, and much
liked by the Children on their bread.
It is more healthy, efpecially if given to
Humors in the blood.

Calves- Take two pair of good Feet
feet and boil the Bones out. Strain
Jelly. it and fkin the
Feet off with Paper:
then add one half pint
of Madeira, two Lemons,
three whites of eggs, fix

144   egg

egg Shells and one half of Sugar. Pour it back and forth until it becomes Clear. Put it in Glaffes to cool.

To make Blew Mange. Lay about one ounce of Ifinglafs in fteep a Day and a Night, then take about a quart of Milk and boyle the Ifinglafs till it jellys, put in fome Cream, a little Rofe-water, a few Bay leaves, and a little Mufk or ambor greafe, boyle it all together till it jellys hard, take it off and ftrain it through a a ftrainer and Power it on a thin Difh and cut it in narrow Pieces and put it on a plate as you think Fitt.

To make Syrup of Rofes. Infufe three pounds of da-mafk Rofe-leaves in a gallon of warm Water, in a well-glazed earthen Pot, with a nar-row Mouth, for eight hours, which ftop fo clofe that none of the Virtue may exhale ; when they have infufed fo long Heat the water again, fqueeze them out, and put in three pounds more of Rofe-leaves, to infufe eight hours More; then prefs them out very hard; then to every quart of this infufion add four pounds of fine fugar, and boil it up to a Syrup.

To Pre-ferve Plumbs an Ele-gant Green. Take eight pounds of Plumbs when a pin will pafs through them, fet them covered with Water, in which a little Alum has been diffolved in a brafs kettle on a hot Hearth to Coddle; they muft be a beautiful Grafs green. Then if you prefer, peel and Coddle again. Diffolve eight pounds of double refined Sugar into a fyrup with a quart of Water. Scum and put in your Plumbs. Then let boil until clear, fcumming often, and they will be of a delectable green. Put them up in Glaffes. Cherries, Apricots, or Grapes, can be done this Way.

To Pre-serve Cherries with the Leaves and Stalks green. Firſt dip the Stalks and leaves in the beſt vinegar boiling Hot, ſtick the ſprig upright in a ſeive till dry. In the mean time boil ſome double-refined ſugar to ſyrup, and Dip the cherries, ſtalks and leaves in the ſyrup, and juſt let them Scald: lay them on a ſeive, and boil them to a candy height, then ſtick the Branches in ſeives and Dry them as you do other ſweetmeats. They look very Pretty at Candle-light in a Deſſert.

To Pre-serve Raſp-berries whole. Take the full weight of your Raſpberries in double refined Sugar beaten and ſifted, lay your Raſpberries ſingle in the Bottom of the Pan; then ſet them on a quick fire 'til all the Sugar be thoroughly  melted: give them two or three Walms, ſcum them, and take them up in glaſſes.

To Pre- Of *Apricocks* take a Pound,
ſerve and a Pound of Sugar, and
Apri- clarifie your Sugar with a Pint
cocks. of Water; and when your Sugar
is made perfect, put it into a Preſerving-
pan and put your *Apricocks* into it, and
ſo let them boyle gently; and when
they bee boyled enough, and your
Syrrup thicke, pot them, and ſo keepe
them.

To Pre- Take your beſt coloured *Pip-*
ſerve *pins* and pare them; then make a
Pippins Piercer and bore a Hole thorow
Red. them: then make Syrrup for
them, as much as will cover them, and
ſo let them boyle, covered cloſe, very
leiſurely, turning them verie often; for
if you turn them not verie often they
will ſpot, and the one Side will not be
like the Other: and let them thus boyle
untill they begin to gelly; then take
them up and pot them, and you may
keepe them all the Yeare.

To Pre- Take faire large Pippins and
ſerve pare them, and Bore a hole
Pippins thorow them as you did for the
white. red ones, then make a weake
Syrup for them, and ſo let them boyle
till they be Tender; then take
them up, and Boyle your
fyrup a little Higher; then
put them in a gally-pot, and
let them Stand all night, and
the next morning, the Syrup
will be ſome what Weaker;
then boyle the fyrup againe to
his ful Thickneſs, and ſo pot them, you
may Keepe them all the Yeare.

If you pleaſe to have them Taſte a
pleaſante taſte, more than the natural
Pippin, put in one graine of Muſke and
one drop of the Chymicall oyle of Cinnamon, and that will make them taſte a
more pleaſant Taſte.

To keep Take Damſons when they
Damſons. are firſt Ripe, pick them off
carefully, Wipe them clean, put them
into Snuff bottles, ſtop them up Tight

fo that no Air can get to them nor Water, but put the bottles into Cold water, hang them over the Fire, let them Heat flowly, let the water boil Slowly for half an Hour, when the water is Cold take out the Bottles and fet them in a cold Place, they will keep twelve Months if they are ftopped Tight. The plumbs muft be Hard.

The American Citron. Take the whole of a large Water-melon (feeds excepted) not too Ripe, cut it into fmall Pieces, take two pounds of loaf Sugar, one pint of water, put it all into a kettle, let it boil Gently for two Hours, then put into Pots for ufe.

To make a Goofe- berry Gam. Gather your Goofeberries full ripe but green; top and tail them and weigh them ; a Pound of Fruit to three quarters of a Pound of double refined Sugar, and half a Pint of Water; boil them till clear and tender, then put it in Pots.

To make Oringe Mar- malad. Take twelve Orinages and four of the peals and Bouil them tender in water to take out the bitternefs, and byle them foe tender you can pull a ftroy through them, and Bett them in a Morter and take the jufe pulp, and putt into your jufe free from the fkin and Seedes, and to a pint of  Jufe a pound of Sugger, lett itt Byle very well, and when it is Byled itt will jelley, and then keep it for your Youfe.

To make Conferve of Hips. Gather Hips before they grow Soft, cut off the Heads and ftalks, flit them in Halves, take out all the Seeds and white that is in them very Clean, then put them into an earthen Pan, and ftir them every Day, or they will grow Mouldy; let them ftand till they are Soft enough to rub them through a coarfe Hair fieve; as the Pulp come, take it off the feive; they are a dry Berry, and will require Pains to rub them through; then add

its

its weight in Sugar, mix them well together without Boiling, and keep it in
Deep gallipots for Ufe.

Black Currant Jelly. Put your black Currants into a preferving pan over the Fire; mafh them with your Spaddle,

and juft let them boil; take them off and Drain them through a very fine Sieve; boil them a quarter of an hour; to every pound of currant Jelly put fourteen ounces of powdered Sugar; boil them ten Minutes; put it in your Pots; let it ftand two Days before you Cover it up, and put brandy Papers over the Jelly before you tie the Papers.

Hartf-horn Jelly. Simmer eight ounces of hartf-horn Shavings with two quarts of Water to one; ftrain it, and boil it with the rinds of four China Oranges, and two lemons pared thin. When Cool add the juice of both, half a

pound

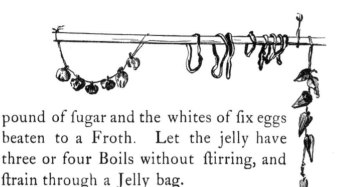

pound of fugar and the whites of fix eggs beaten to a Froth. Let the jelly have three or four Boils without ftirring, and ftrain through a Jelly bag.

Of Pickling.

To pickle Cucum-bers green. Wafh them and Dry them in a Cloth; then take water, vinegar, falt, fennel tops, dill-tops, and a little mace; make it Sharp enough for tafte; then Boil it awhile, then take it off and let it Stand till cold; then put in the Cucumbers and ftop the Veffel clofe, and within a week they will be Fit for ufe.

The Pickle. Take a gallon of the beft Vinegar, with one quart of Water and a handful of Salt, an ounce of Pepper, boil them and let ftand till

Cold

Cold, then take a quarter of a pound of Ginger, falt it cut in pieces and let ftand a Week : take half a pound of Muftard-feed, wafh and lay to Dry. When dry, bruife half of it ; now lay a row of Cabbage, a row of Cauliflower and Beans,

and throw betwixt every row, your muftard-feed, fome black pepper, fome Jamaica pepper, fome ginger, mix an ounce of the root of Tumerick powdered ; put it in the Pickle which muft go over all. It is beft when it hath been made two years, though it may be ufed the Firft year.

To pickle the fine Purple Cabbage fo much admired at the great Tables. Take two Cauliflower, two red Cabbages, half a peck of kidney-Beans, fix fticks, with fix cloves of Garlic on each ftick : wafh all well, give them one Boil up, then drain them on a Sieve, and lay them Leaf by Leaf upon a large Table, and falt them with bay-falt : then lay

154   them

them a drying in the fun, until as dry
as cork.

To pickle   Make a ftrong Pickle, with
Radiſh- cold fpring-water and bay-falt,
Pods.   ftrong enough to bear an Egg.
then put your Pods in and lay a thin
Board on them to keep them under
Water, let them ftand ten Days, then
Drain them in a Sieve and
lay them on a Cloth to dry ;
then take white-wine Vinegar as much as you think
will Cover them, boil it and
put your Pods in a jar, with
Ginger, Mace and Jamaica pepper, Pour
your vinegar boiling Hot on and cover
them with a coarfe Cloth, let them ftand
two Days ; repeat this two or three
times. When cold cover it Clofe.

To pickle   Set fpring-water on the Fire,
Fennel. with a handful of Salt : when it
boils, tie your Fennel in bunches, and
put them in the Water, juft give them a
Scald, lay them on a cloth to Dry :

        when

when cold put in a Glafs, with a little mace and nutmeg, fill it with cold Vinegar, lay a bit of green Fennel on top, and over that a Bladder and leather.

To pickle Samphire. Pick your Samphire from dead or withered Branches; lay it in a Bell metal or Brafs Pot;

then put in a pint of water, and a pint of Vinegar; fo do till your pickle is an inch above your Samphire; have a lid fit for the Pot, and pafte it clofe down, that no fteam may go out; Keep it boiling an Hour, take it off and cover it with old Sacks or any old cloths, all about the Pot; When it is cold, put it up in Tubs or Pots, the beft by itfelf. The Vinegar ufed muft be the beft.

To pickle Walnuts to eat like Mangoes. Take green Walnuts, before the Shell has grown to any Hardnefs in them; pick them from the ftalk and put them in

cold

cold Water, and fet them on a gentle Fire, till the outward fkins begin to Peel off; then, with a coarfe cloth, wipe it off; then put them into a Jar, and put water and falt Therein, fhifting it once a day for ten days, till the bitternefs and difcolouring of the Water be gone; then take a good Quantity of muftard feed, which beat up with Vinegar, till it becomes Coarfe muftard; then take fome clove of Garlick, fome Ginger, and a little Cloves and Mace; make a hole in each nut, and put in a little of this; then take white wine Vinegar, and boil them Together, which put to the Nuts boiling hot, with fome pepper, ginger, cloves and mace, as alfo, fome of the muftard feed and garlick, which keep clofe ftopped for Ufe.

To pickle Naftur- tium Buds. Gather your little Nubs quickly after the Blofloms are off. Put them in cold water and Salt three Days, fhifting them

157

them once a Day : then make a pickle for
them (don't boil them at all) of fome
white wine, fome white wine vinegar,
Shalot Horfe-Radifh, whole pepper and
fald, and a Blade or two of Mace : then
put in your feeds and ftop them clofe up.
They are to be eaten as Capers.

Of Beverages.

"For to keep your ftomach warm,
    A moderate glafs can do no harm."

Some
Hints
about
Coffee.
If the Hob is too hot the
Coffee will never clear. The
Receipts that are
given in the
Cookery books com-
pletely Drive off the flavour of the Berry by the
length of Time it is told
to be Boiled. Flower of
Muftard, a tablefpoonful to the ounce is
thought by fome to improve the Flavour. Coffee made before hand and

158   Heated

Heated up is ever a Vile flop, detefted by every Coffee drinker and every one elfe who has the Tafte of his Mouth.

As Subftitutes for Coffee, fome ufe dry brown Bread crufts and roaft them. Others foak Rye grain in Rum and Roaft it. Where there is a large family of Apprentices and Workmen it may be worth while to ufe the fubftitutes or mix them Half and Half with coffee, but after all the beft Economy is to go without.

Orgeat. Pound three Ounces of fweet and fix fingle Bitter almonds, add one Pint of water, Strain through a lawn Sieve, and then add two tablefpoonfuls of Orange flower water.

Rafp-berry Vinegar. To a market Gallon of Rafp-berries take a gallon of Common vinegar, put it into an Earthen pan, and let it Stand three

Days; then Strain it through a Flannel bag, turning back the Juice until it runs Bright; and to every Quart of juice take a quart of Clarified Sugar, Boil it till it Snaps, put in your juice and boil it one Minute, take off the Scum, put it into a Stone bottle, and it will Keep if neceffary, two Years.

Switchels or Hay-maker's Drinks. Mix Ginger, Vinegar, Molaffes, and what Water you will, according to Tafte.

Tama-rind Water. Boil three Pints of Water with an Ounce and a Half of Tamarinds, three ounces of Cur-

rants, and two Ounces of ftoned Raifins, till near a third be con-fumed. Strain it on a Bit of Lemon-peel, which Remove in an hour, as it gives a Bitter tafte if left too long. A delightful Beverage.

Verjuice. Gather fome Ripe Crab-apples, and lay them in a Heap to Sweat; then throw away the Stalks, and having Mafhed the fruit Exprefs the Juice: ftrain it and in a Month it will be Ready.

Mint Put into a Tumbler about *Julep.* a Dozen fprigs of the Tender fhoots of Mint; upon them put a Spoonful of white Sugar, an equal proportion of Peach and common Brandy, fo as to fill up one Third, or perhaps a little Lefs. Then take Rafped or pounded Ice, and fill up the Tumbler; Epicures Rub the lips of the Tumbler with a piece of Frefh Pineapple, and the Tumbler itfelf is very often Incrufted outfide with Stalactites of Ice. As the Ice Melts, you Drink.

Treacle- Boil, for twenty Minutes, *Beer a* three Pounds of molaffes, in *Table* from Six to Eight gallons of *Beer.* Soft water, with a Handful of

Hops tied in a Muflin rag, or a little Extract of Gentian. When cooled in the Tub, add a Pint of good Beer-yeaft, or from four to fix Quarts of Frefh Worts from the brewer's Vat. Cover the Beer (and all Fermenting liquids) with Blankets or coarfe Cloths. Pour it from the Lees and Bottle it. You may ufe Sugar for Molaffes, which is Lighter.

For Brewing Spruice Beer. Take four Ounces Hops, boil half an Hour in one Gallon water, Strain it, then add fixteen Gallons Warm water,  two gallons Molaffes, eight Ounces effence Spruice diffolved in one quart Water, put it in a Clean Cafk, Shake it well together, add half pint Emptins, let it Stand and Work one Week, if very warm Weather lefs time will Do, when Drawn off add one fpoonful of Molaffes to each Bottle.

Spring Beer. Take a Bunch of Sarfaparilla, Sweet Fern, Wintergreen, Saffafras, Burdock Root, Cumfrey Root, Nettle Root, Spice Bufh, Solomon's Seal, Black Birch, 3 Ounces of Hops 3 raw Potatoes, pared and fliced. Boil together in 4 Gallons of Water for 6 Hours; ftrain and add a Quart of Molaffes to 3 Gallons of Beer. To have the *Beer* very rich, brown half a Pound of Bread and add to the Liquor. If the Liquor is too thick, dilute with cold Water. When luke-warm, put in a Pint of frefh lyvile Yeaft. Place in a temperate Situation, covered, but not too clofely. After Fermentation, bottle it clofe, or keep in tight Keg.

To make Ebulum or Elder Berry Wine. Take five quarts of Elder berry juice and three Gallons of Water and Twelve pounds of good Brown fugar: mix them all well and Boyl them together and fcum it as long as any Scum arifes.

163   When

When it is almoſt cold, work it with
yearſt a day or two, and when it hath done
Working put it into a Caſk, and in
March when it is Fine, bottle it after it
is Strained through a Woolen Bagg.

L'Eau de " Grown Old, and grown Stu-
la Vie.   pid, you juſt think me Fit
To tranſcribe from my Grandmother's
     book a Receipt ;
And Comfort it is for a Wight in Diſ-
     treſs,
To be ſtill of ſome Uſe : he could Scarce
     be of Leſs.
Were greater his Talents, fair Anne
     might command
His head if more Worth than his Heart
     or his hand.
Your Mandates obeying, he Sends with
     much glee,
The Genuine Receipt to make *l'Eau de
la Vie.*"
   Take ſeven large Oranges, and Pare
     them as thin
As a Wafer, or What is much Thinner,
     your Skin,

Six Ounces of Sugar, next take, and
bear Mind,
That the Sugar be of the Beſt Double-
refined.

Clear the Sugar in near half a Pint of
ſpring-water,
In the Neat ſilver Saucepan you Bought
for your Daughter.
Then the Fourth of a Pint, you muſt
Fully allow,
Of new Milk, made as Warm as it Comes
from the Cow.
Put the Rinds of the Lemons, the Milk,
and the Syrup,
In a Jar, with the Rum, and Give them
a ſtir up.

A full quart of Old Rum (French
    Brandy is better,
But we ne'er in Receipts, fhould Stick
    clofe to the Letter;)
And then, to your Tafte, you may Add
    fome Perfume,
Goa-ftone, or Whatever you like in its
    Room.
Let it ftand thus ten Days, but Remem-
    ber to fhake it,
And the Clofer you Stop it, the richer
    you Make it.
Then filter through Paper, 't will fparkle
    and Rife,
Be as Soft as your Lips, and as Bright as
    your Eyes.
Laft, bottle it up, and Believe me, the
    Vicar
Of E— himfelf never Drank better
    Liquor.
In a word, it Excels, by a million of
    Odds,
The nectar your Sifter prefents to the
    Gods !

Capillaire or Syrup of Maiden Hair. Put seven Pounds of common Lump sugar into a Pan, add Thereunto seven pints of Water, Boil it well, and keep Skimming it : then take the White of an Egg, put it in some Water, and beat it up well with a Whisk: take the Froth off and scatter it therein, and keep it Skimming until it is quite clear; then add thereto Half a pint of orange-flower Water. When well Mixed and Cold put it into a stone Bottle for use; the bottle must be Dry and Clean or it will Mother.

Mead or Metheglin. Take ten Gallons of water, and two Gallons of Honey, a handful of Raced ginger : then take two lemons, cut them in Peaces and put them into it, Boil it very well, keep it Skimming: let it Stand all Night in the same Vessel you Boil it in, the next Morning barrel it up with Barm. About a Month after you may Bottle it.

To

To make Cordial Poppy Water. Take two Gallons of very good Brandy and a peck of Poppies, and put them together in a Wide mouthed Glaſs, and let them Stand forty-eight Hours, and then Strain the Poppies out: take a pound of Raiſins of the ſun, ſtone them, and an Ounce of Coriander ſeeds, an ounce of ſweet-Fennel ſeeds, and an ounce of Liquorice ſliced. Bruiſe them all To-gether, and put them into the Brandy, with a Pound of good powder Sugar; and then let them Stand four or Eight weeks, Shaking it every Day: and then ſtrain it off, and Bottle for Uſe.

Uſque-baugh. Take Three gallons of Strong rectified Spirits, half a Gallon of Rich ſweet Engliſh Wine, four pounds of Raiſins, the ſun-dried ſtoned: ſix Nutmegs, two ounces of Mace, four ounces of Cinnamon, one ounce of Cloves, one ounce of Coriander ſeed, and one ounce of Ginger: Steep the whole

168

whole for a Fortnight in the Spirits, then put the Raisins and half a pound of stick Liquorice in a gallon of Soft Water and let it Boyle till it be Half a gallon; then put it through a Sieve, and dissolve eighteen pounds of Loaf sugar in a Mortar, with half a pint of Spirits of Wine, an ounce of Oil of Cloves, bray it until the oil Disappears, and it is Fit to Barrel. To make it a fine Yellow use a little Saffron steeped in Water and put it to the Liquor : Fine it with Allum Water.

Cherry Bounce. Mix together six Pounds of Ripe morellas and six Pounds of large Black heart Cherries. Put them into a wooden Bowl or Tub, and with a Pestle or Mallet Mash them so as to Crack all the Stones.

Mix with the Cherries, three pounds of Loaf-sugar, or of Sugar Candy broken up, and put them into a Demijohn, or into a Large stone Jar. Pour on two

gallons

gallons of the beſt Double Rectified Whiſkey. Stop the Veſſel cloſely, and let it Stand three Months, ſhaking it Every Day during the firſt Month. At the End of the three Months you may Strain the liquor and Bottle it off. It Improves by Age.

Cool Tankard or Beer Cup. A quart of Mild Ale, a glaſs of white Wine, one of Brandy, one of Capillaire, the juice of a Lemon, a roll of the Peel pared thin, Nutmeg grated on the top (a ſprig of Borrage or Balm) and a bit of toaſted Bread.

Cider Cup is the ſame, only ſubſtituting Cider.

Ratafia. Blanch two Ounces of peach and apricot Kernels, Bruiſe and put them into a Bottle, and Fill nearly up with brandy. Diſſolve half a pound of white Sugar candy in a Cup of Cold Water, and Add to the Brandy after it has Stood a month on the Kernals, and

they

they are Strained off; then Filter through Paper and Bottle for Ufe.

Tea Punch. Hot tea two Pints; Arrack thirteen Ounces; Sugar four ounces; Flavoured by Rubbing off the Yellow peel of the lemons, or Green Tea, Juniper and Champagne.

Milk Punch. Take two gallons and a half of French Brandy, and infufe in it for one Night the outer rind of fifteen lemons, and as Many oranges pared very Thin. Add to it the before-mentioned Quantity of Fruit, and fif-

teen Quarts of cold water that has been Boiled, feven pounds and a half of fine loaf Sugar, and half a Pint of milk, let them be Mixed and Stand till cold, then add a Bottle of Jamaica Rum, put it into a Cafk the proper fize and

Stop it up clofe for a Month or fix Weeks.

N. B. Take out the Lemon and Orange peel before you Add the Fruit.

Egg Nog, or Auld Man's Milk. Beat the yolks and Whites of fix Eggs Separately. Put to the beat Yolks, fugar and a Quart of new Milk, or thin Cream. Add to this Rum, Whifky, or Brandy to tafte (about a half Pint) Slip in the Whipped whites, and give the whole a Gentle Stir up in the china Punch Bowl, in which it fhould be Mixed. It may be Flavored with Nutmeg or Lemon-zeft.

Lambs Woole. Goode ale, high Spiced and Sea-foned, mingled withe Roafted Apples and Toafte.

Waffail Bowle. Ye fhal take a Guide meafure of Milde Ale, not ye Strengeft, and mingle with high Spices, well

Sweeten,

Sweeten, alfo Toafte, and the Eggs of Fowle if it be to youre Minde, and Seething Hot.

Flip. Keep grated Ginger and Nutmeg with a fine dried Lemon Peel, rubbed together in a mortar. To make a quart of Flip : Put the Ale on the fire to warm, and beat up three or four Eggs with four ounces of moift Sugar, a teafpoonful of grated Nutmeg or Ginger and a quartern of good old Rum or Brandy. When the Ale is near to boil, put it into one pitcher, and the Rum and Eggs, etc. into another : turn it from one Pitcher to another till it is as fmooth as cream. To heat plunge in red hot Loggerhead or Poker.

N. B. This quantity I ftyled *One Yard of Flannel.*

Obs. The above is given in the words of the Publican who gave us the Receipt.

Mulled

Mulled Wine. Boil the fpiceries (Cinnamon, Nutmeg grated, Cloves, and Mace, in any quantity Approved, in a Quarter-pint or better of Water ; put to this a full pint of Port, with fugar to Tafte. Mix it Well. Serve hot with Toafts or Rufk. The yolks of Eggs were Formerly mixed with Mulled wine, as in making Cuftard or Egg-Caudle, and many Flavoring ingredients were Employed which are now Difcarded.

Sack Poffet. Put ¾ lb. of white Sugar into a pt. of Canary Wine. Strain into this the beaten Whites and Yolks of 15 Eggs. Place over Fire until fcald-

ing hot. Add 1 qt. boiling Milk with little grated Nutmeg. In pouring Milk into Eggs and Wine, hold Hand very high and ftir conftantly. Set before Fire ½ Hour. Serve.

Ancient A Quart of Red Wine, an
Ypocras. ounce of Cinnamon, half an
ounce of Ginger, a Quarter of an ounce
of Pepper, all put in a Bag and Infufed
in the Wine.

Clary or Claret mingled
Night- with Honey and
Cap. Aromatics.
    A favorite Compofing
Draught of the Sixteenth
Century.

Tewah- A pint of Table Beer (or Ale,
diddle. if you intend it for a fupple-
ment to your "Night-Cap,") a tablefpoonful of Brandy and a tea fpoonful
of brown Sugar ; a little grated Nutmeg
or Ginger may be added, and a roll of
very thin Cut Lemon Peel.

            Obs.   Before   our
            readers make any re-
            marks on this Com-
            pofition, we beg of
them to tafte it ; if the materials are
good and their Palate vibrates in Unifon

with our own, they will find it one of
the Pleasanteſt beverages they ever put
to their Lips, and as Lord Ruthven
ſays, " This is a right Goſſip's Cup that
far exceeds all the Ale that ever Mother
Bunch made in her life time."

On the Improvement of Female Beauty.

Fixing A very ingenious Mode is
the per- employed for fixing the per-
fume of fumes of Plants in expreſſed
Flowers. Oil without the aſſiſtance of
any but the gentleſt Heat. The oil
uſed is either oil of bhen, or the pureſt
olive oil. The flowers whoſe aroma is

 to be extracted are
thickly ſpread upon
flakes of Wool, pre-
viouſly ſoaked in the
Oil; then they are
encloſed in tin Boxes,
and ſuffered to remain till the Flowers begin to decay, and loſe their Colour
176 and

and Texture. They are then removed, frefh flowers are added, and the Maceration repeated till the oil becomes richly Impregnated with the Scent of the flower ufed. This oil is then Put into a ftill with Water, and the Effential oil comes over with the Water; or the wool is preffed, and the fragrant oil feparated from the flowers is put into clofe-Stopped bottles.

A hand-fome Scent. There is a little Beaft called a Mufkquafh that liveth in fmall Houfes in the Ponds like Mole Hills. Their Cods fcent as fweet and as ftrong as Mufk, and will laft a long time handfomely wrapped in Cotton wool. They are very good to lay amongft Cloaths. Their Cods fcent ftrongeft in May.

Rofe Water. Take of the leaves of frefh damafk Rofes, with the heels cut off, fix pounds: Water to prevent burning. Diftil off a Gallon.

Cologne Water. Of alcohol, one Gallon : oil of Lavender, twelve drachms : oil of Rofemary, four drachms : effence of Lemon twelve drachms : oil of Bergamot, twelve drachms : oil of Cinnamon, twelve drops.

Hungary Water. To one pint of highly rectified Spirit of Wine, put an ounce  of oil of Rofemary, and two drams effence of Ambergris, fhake the bottle well feveral Times, then let the Cork out for twenty-four hours. After a Month, during which fhake it Daily, put it in fmall bottles. Leave out the Rofemary and it is Honey Water.

Lavender Water. Take a pint of highly rectified fpirit of wine, one ounce of effential oil of Lavender, two drams effence of Ambergris. Put all into a quart Bottle and fhake extremely Well.

Pearl Powder for the Face. The fineſt is made from real Pearls, and is the leaſt hurtful to the Skin, but it is too dear for common Uſe.

To turn Red Hair Black. Should one be ſo afflicted as to have red Hair it may be dyed black in this manner. Take a pint of the liquor of pickled Herrings, half a pound of Lamp black, and two ounces of the ruſt of Iron. Mix, boil and Strain them, then rub the liquid well into the roots of the Hair.

Turkiſh Rouge or Secret of the Seraglio. Infuſe, for three or four days, in a bottle of the fineſt white wine vinegar, half a pound of Brazil wood, of a golden red Color, well pounded in a Mortar, Boil them together half an hour, ſtrain them through a Linen, and place

the

the Liquid again over the Fire. In the 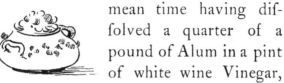 mean time having dif-folved a quarter of a pound of Alum in a pint of white wine Vinegar, mix the two liquids well Together with a Spatula. The fcum which now arifes on being Carefully taken off and gradually Dried, will prove a moft Beautiful, deli-cate and perfectly Inoffenfive rouge or Carmine.

Vegeta-- Take marine Marfh-Mallow
ble roots, cut them into lengths of
Tooth five or fix inches, and of the
Brufhes. thicknefs of middling rattan
Cane. Dry them in the Shade. Next finely pulverize two ounces of good Dragons blood, and with four ounces of Spirit and half an ounce of frefh conferve of Rofes, fet over a Charcoal fire. When Dragons blood is diffolved put in about thirty of the Marfhmallow fticks, ftir them about that all Parts may abforb the Dye.

Both ends of the Sticks fhould previous

vious to immerfion be Bruifed gently by a Hammer fo as to open its Fibres, and thereby form a Brufh.

Ufed by dipping one of the ends in Powder or opiate, and rubbing againft the Teeth, which they cleanfe and whiten Admirably.

An Oint- Take two Ounces
ment to of Boars greafe, one
caufe Drachm
Hair to of the
Grow. Afhes of
burnt Bees, one
Drachm of the
Afhes of Southernwood, one
Drachm of the Juice of a white
Dilly root, one Drachm of
pure mufk : and according to
Art, make an Ointment of
these ; and the Day before
the full Moon fhave the Place and anoint it every Day with this ointment. It will caufe Hair to grow where you 'll have it.

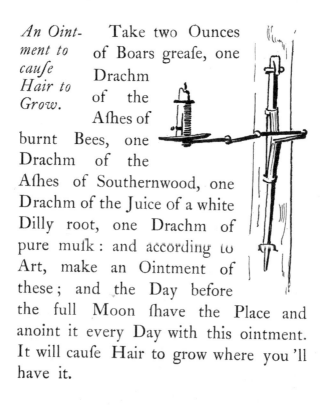

Bando-line. Take Quince feeds and cover them with Water. When it will be found that a Gummy fubftance will exude from them, ufeful in holding the Hair in Waves, or in making the Beau catchers adhere to the Head.

Sperma-cetti Oint-ment. Melt one drachm of white Wax, one of Spermacetti, and two ounces of Olive Oil; and two ounces of Rofe water, and half an ounce of Orange-flower water. Beat to a Cream while cooling.

To Whiten and Clean the Hands. Boil a quart of new milk and turn it with a pint of Aqua-vitæ. Then take off the Curd, then put into the Poffet a Pint of Rhenifh wine, and that will raife another Curd, which take off; then put in the whites of fix eggs well beaten, and that will raife another Curd, which you muft take off, and mix the three Curds together very well, and put them into a Gallipot, and put the

Poffet into a Bottle. Scour your Hands with the Curd, and wafh them with the Poffet.

To Pro-cure a good Colour. Take Germander, Rue, Fennitory of each a good Handful, one Pennyworth of Saffron tied up in a rag, half a pound of blue Currants bruifed, ftamp the Herbs, and infufe all thefe ingredients in three Pints of fack over a gentle Fire til half be confumed, drink a quarter of a Pint Morning and Evening, and walk after it; Repeat this quantity once or twice.

To Cure a Pimpled Face, and Sweeten the Blood. Take Sena one Ounce, put it in a fmall Pot and pour a quart or more of boiling Water on it; then put as many Prunes as you can get in. Cover it with Paper and fet in the Oven with Houfehold bread and take of  this every day according as it operates. Continue this always or at leaft half a year.

Ma-
conba
Snuff.
The varied flavour of Snuffs of different kinds arifes lefs from the state of the original Leaf, than the factitious additions of Manufacturers.

The fnuff of Martinico, celebrated under the term " Maconba," is made from the beft leaves, which being moiftened with Juice from their excellent Sugar canes, undergoes fermentation, and having thrown off the offenfive Fetor in fcum and refiduum is Evaporated and ground in the ufual Manner.

A good
Thing
to Wafh
the
Face in.
Take a large piece of Camphire, the quantity of a Goofe-Egg, and break it fo that it will go into a Pint Bottle, which fill with water ; when it has ftood a month, put a Spoonful of it in three Spoonfuls of Milk and wafh in it.

Wear a Piece of Lead, beaten exceeding thin, for a Forehead piece, under a Forehead-cloth ; it keeps the Forehead fmooth and plump.

184   *To*

To take off Freckles. Take Bean flower Water or Elder-flower Water, or May Dew gathered from Corn, of either the quantity of four Spoonfuls, and add to it one Spoonful of Oil of Tartar very new drawn; mix it well together, and often wafh the Face with it.

For Chopped Hands. Boiled potatoes are faid to Cleanfe the Hands as well as Common Soap; they prevent chops in the winter feafon and keep the fkin foft and healthy.

APPROVED SECRETS IN PHYSICKE AND CHIRURGERY.

Obferva-tions. The gracious acceptance of the Widows Offering Encourrages me to caft my Mite into the Treafury and publifh a Treatife to lead the poorer fort into the Pleafant Paths

of

of Health, and as it is defigned for thofe who cannot Afford to dye by the Hand

 of a Doctor, I hope that the Legitimate fons of Efculapius will be the more Merciful. But as for the fpurious Breed they have no right to find fault with what they can't Mend and t'will be prudent to make a Secret of their own Ignorence.

For any The Turpentine that iffueth
Ach. from the cones of the *Larch Tree* is fingularly good to heal Wounds, and to draw out the Malice of any Ach: rubbing the Place therewith and throwing upon it the Powder of Sage-leaves.

For The Tar that is made of all
Stitches. forts of Pitch wood is an excellent Thing to take away thofe desperate Stitches of the Sides which perpetually afflicteth thofe poor People that are ftricken with the Plague of the Back.

Note. — You muft take a large Toaft

or Cake, flit and dip it in the Tar, and
bind it warm to the Side.

Small   Take of Balm, Mint, Hart's
Snail   Tongue, Ground ivy, Flowers
Water. of the dead nettle, Mallow flowers, Elder flowers, a handful : Snails, freed
from their Shells, and whites of Eggs each
four ounces; nutmegs half an ounce :
milk one Gallon. Diftil in a Water bath
to drynefs.

Vapours   Some of the Symptoms are,
and   a Thumping at the Heart, a
Hyfteric Croaking of the Guts and a Ful-
Fits.   nefs of the Stomach. She has a
great Heavinefs and Di-
jection of Spirit, and a
Cloud feems to hang
upon all her Senfes. She
is continually out of Humor, she knows
not Why, and out of Order, fhe knows
not Where. In the firft place I would
have her Stomach cleanfed with a vomit
of Indian Phyfic.

The Reſt of the cure can be preformed by an exact Obſervation of the following Rules : —

Endeavor to preſerve a Cheerful ſpirit, putting the beſt Conſtruction on Everybodys Words and Behavior.

Plunge three mornings every week into cold water, which will rouſe the Sluggiſh Spirits ſurpriſingly. Stir Nimbly about your affairs.

I forbid all ſorts of Drams  which will riſe the Spirits only to ſink them, nor do I allow one Pinch of Snuff or one drop of Bohea Tea, which makes people very Lumpiſh and Miſerable. Nor muſt ſhe eat one morſel of Beef which inclines People too much to Hang themſelves. She muſt ſuffer none of the Diſturbances and Diſappointments of an Empty world to prey upon her Mind or ruffle her ſweet Temper. She muſt be cheerful in Spite of a Churliſh Huſband or Cloudy Weather.

For

For the Kings Evil. Take two Toades, and let them faſt two or three dayes, then Boyle them in a pint of Oyle in a new pipkin covered ſo long, till they be brought to a Black coal broken in Peeces. Preſſe out the Oyle, from the ſaid Toades, reſerve a fourth part, to the other three parts add halfe a Pound of yellow 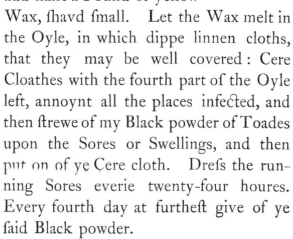 Wax, ſhavd ſmall. Let the Wax melt in the Oyle, in which dippe linnen cloths, that they may be well covered : Cere Cloathes with the fourth part of the Oyle left, annoynt all the places infected, and then ſtrewe of my Black powder of Toades upon the Sores or Swellings, and then put on of ye Cere cloth. Dreſs the running Sores everie twenty-four houres. Every fourth day at furtheſt give of ye ſaid Black powder.

The Rattle Snake. The Rattle Snake who Poyſons with a Vapour that comes thorough two crooked Fangs in their Mouth: the Indians when weary with

189　　　　travelling

travelling lay hold with one hand behind their Head, with the other taking hold of the Tail, with their teeth tear off the ſkin of their Back and feed upon them alive : which greatly refreſhes them, they have Leafs of Fat in their Bellies, which is excellent for to annoint frozen Limbs, and for aches wondrous foveraign. Their Hearts ſwallowed freſh is an Antidote againſt their venome and their Liver bruiſed and applied to their Bite is a preſent Remedy.

Strange Cure for Wolf in the Breaſt. A Drummer's wife much afflicted with Wolf in the Breaſt for ſome time ſuaged the pain by bathing it with ſtrong Malt Beer which it would Suck in greedily as ſome living Creature : when ſhe could come by no more Beer, ſhe made uſe of Rhum, a ſtrong Water drawn from Sugar Canes, with which it was lull'd a Sleep. At laſt

ſhe

ſhe put a Quantity of Arſnick to the Rhum, and bathing of it as formerly, ſhe utterly Deſtroyed it, and Cured her ſelf: but her kind Huſband who ſucked out the Poyſon as the Sore was healing loſt all his Teeth, but without further danger.

For Paines in yᵉ Breſt or Sinnues. Weare a Wilde Catts skin on ye Place grieved.

For Indi-geſtion. A good quantity of Old Cheeſe is the beſt Thing to eat when diſtreſſed by eating too much Fruit or oppreſſed with any kind of Food. Phyſicians give it in Caſes of extreme Danger.

A Rem-edy for Pain of the Stomach. The Skin of a Gripe dreſt with the Down on is good to wear upon the Stomach for the Pain and Coldneſs of it.

For Madneſſe. Take yᵉ herbe Hypericon and boile it in Water or drinke, untill it be Strong of it, and redd in
191   colour;

colour ; or elſe putt a Bundle of it in new drinke to worke, and give it yᵉ Patient to drinke, permitting him to drinke Nothing elſe. Firſt purge him well with two or three feeds of Spurge. Let them not eat much, but Keepe dyet, and ye ſhall ſee Wondrous Effects in fewe dayes. I haue knowne it to cure perfectly to admiration in five dayes.

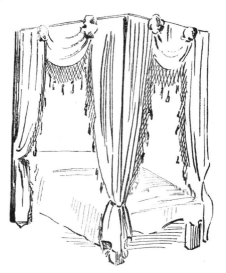

For Yᵉ Falling Sickneſſe. Purge firſt with yᵉ Extract of Hellebore, and uſe meadow Cinquefoile, and God Willing he ſhall be Perfectly cured in Short

or

Loading for B'ar.

or longer tyme, according as the Difeafe hath taken roote. Care fhould be taken to Calm the Spirits of the Patient, and keep them from running Riot in an un-happy Manner. For that Intention bleed him and then burn Feathers under his Nofe or elfe Leather or the Hoofs of any Animal.

When Crooked and Lame and full of Pain. To lye upon Bear Skins newly flead off, and with fome upon one until he fweat, every night, is a Gallant remedy. Anointing with Bears Greafe will harden one to the Cold, and is good for Aches and Cold Swellings.

A purg-ing Diet-drink in the Spring. Take fix gallons of Ale, three ounces of Rhubarb, twelve ounces of Senna, twelve ounces of Madder-root, twelve ounces of Dock-root, twelve handfuls of Scabius, twelve handfuls of Agrimony, three ounces of Anifeeds; flice and cut thefe, put them in a Bag and let them Work in ale. Drink of it three or four times a Day.

Drafts or Poul-tices. Mix well together one pound of Linfeed-Meal and a pint of Ale yeaft. Expofe this Cataplafm to a gentle heat. Take a Flapjack and Sprinkle well with muftard and Apply.

Bread boiled in Milk is a good ordinary Poultice; it may be made a ftimulating Draft by ufing vinegar, or adding Horferadifh, garlick, or muftard.

To make Children cut their Teeth eafy. Take the Brains of a Hare, or the Brains of a Hen, and rub the Child's Gums with them, once or twice a Day, and it will make the Teeth cut without Pain.

Another.

Another. Take a Tooth out of a Calves Head and hang it about the Neck of the Child.

Tic Do-loreux. This dreadful Difeafe is treated by Strengthening the general fyftem by tonics. Mefmerifm or Fafcination is the only One that promifes much Relief.

For Tooth Ache. The Beaks of the Ofprey excell for the Tooth-ach, picking the Gums therewith till they bleed.

Inflammation of the Throat. A fwallow's Neft ftamped (the infide) and Applied to the throat outwardly will allay an Inflammation.

The Bloody-Flux Cured. A Gentleman of good quality living fometime in Virginia was fore Troubled for a long time with the Bloody-Flux, having tried feveral Remedies without any good Effect, at laft was induced with a longing

195   Defire

Defire to drink the Fat Drippings of
a Goofe newly taken from
the fire, which abfolutely
Cured him, who was in Dif-
pair of ever recovering his
Health again. To prevent
this Difeafe avoid fleeping on
the Cold ground and wading
in Cold Water. Never eat
immoderately of any fort of
Fruit, nor venture to drink new or foul
Cider by any means.

An Eafy   *A Cold in the Head.* **Pare**
and   very thin the Yellow rind of an
Natural   orange, Roll it up infide out,
method   and Thruft a roll into each
of Curing   Noftril.

   A Cold. Drink a pint of Cold water,
lying down in Bed.

   A Burn or Scald. Immediately plunge
the Part into cold water, Keep it in an
Hour if not well before.

   A Bruife. Immediately apply Treacle
on a piece of Brown Paper.

   The Afthma. Take a Pint of cold
water

water every night as you lie down in
Bed.

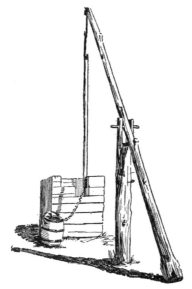

Bleeding at the Nofe. To prevent
drink Whey largely every Morning and
eat Raifins much.

Deafnefs. Be Electrified thro' the Ear.

Chin-Cough or Hooping Cough. Rub
the feet thoroughly with Hog's lard before the Fire at going to Bed and keep
the Child warm therein.

Apoplexy. To prevent ufe the Cold
bath and drink only Water.

For

For the Hickup. Take three or four preferved Damfons in your mouth at a Time and fwollow them by Degrees.

A Stitch in the Side. Apply Treacle fpread on a hot Toaft.

An Achar-ifton for the Scurvey. The tops of Green Spruce Bougs boyled in Bear, and drunk, is affuredly a Gallant Remedy for the Scurvey : they alfo make a Lotion of the decoction, adding Hony and Allum.

Nota benè. No man can with a good Con-fcience take a Fee or a reward before ye Partie receive benefit Apparent : and then he is not to Demand anything, but what God fhall putt into the heart of the Partie to give him. And he is not to Refufe anything, that fhall be fo Given him, for it comes from God.

A man is not to Neglect that partie, to whom he hath once Adminiftred, but to vifit him at leaft once a Day, and to medle with no more than he can well Attend.

PALATABLE DISHES FOR THE INDIS-
POSED.

Direc- tions for the Sick.   I do not pretend to meddle here in the Phyfical Way : but a few Directions for the Cook or Nurfe I prefume will not be improper, to make fuch a Diet, &c. as the Doctor fhall order.

A very Support- ing Broth againft any kind of weak- nefs.   Boil two Pounds of Loin of Mutton, with a very large Handful of Chervil, in two Quarts of Water to one. Take off part of the Fat. Any other Herb or Root may be added. Take half a pint two or three times a Day.

Panada. Set a little Water on the fire with a glafs of white wine, fome fugar and a Scrape of nutmeg and lemon-peel : meanwhile grate fome crumbs of Bread. The moment the mixture boils up, keeping it ftill on the Fire, put the
crumbs

crumbs in, and let it Boil as faſt as it can. When of a proper thickneſs to Drink, take it off.

To make Sage-Tea. Take a little Sage, a little Baum, put it in a pan, ſlice a Lemon, a few knobs of Sugar, one glaſs of white wine, pour on theſe two or three Quarts of boiling water, cover it and Drink when thirſty; when ſtrong enough take out the Herbs.

Egg in Tea. An Egg broken into a cup of Tea makes a Breakfaſt more Supporting than tea if Taken Alone.

Artificial Asses Milk. Boil two ounces of Hartſhorn ſhavings, two ounces of Pearl Barley, two ounces of candied Eringo root, and one dozen of Snails, that have been Bruiſed in two quarts of Water, to one, mix with an equal quantity of new Milk, when taken twice a Day.

To

To make the Pec- toral Drink. Take a gallon of Water and half a pound of Pearl-barley, boil it with a quarter of a pound of Figs fplit, a pennyworth of liquorice fliced to pieces, a quarter of a pound of Raifins of the fun ftoned; boil all together till half is Wafted, then ftrain it off. This is ordered in the Meafles, and feveral other Diforders for a Drink.

To make Barley Water. Take of Pearl Barley, four ounces, put it in a large Pipkin, and cover it with Water; when the Barley is thick and tender, put it in more Water and boil it up again, and fo do till 'tis of a good Thicknefs to drink: then put in a Blade or two of Mace or a Stick of Cinnamon. Let it have a warm or two and ftrain it out and fqueeze in the Juice of two or three Lemons and a bit

of

of Peel, and fweeten it to your Tafte with fine Sugar ; let it ftand till 'tis cold, and then run it thro' a Bag and bottle it out, it will keep three or four Days.

To boil Salop. It is a hard Stone ground to powder. Take a large teafpoonful of the Powder and put it into a pint of boiling Water, keep Stirring it till it is like a fine Jelly, then put in wine and fugar to your Palate, and Lemon if it will agree.

Milk Porridge. Prepare a fine Gruel of fplit Grits, ftrain it, and then add a Sufficiency of milk and ferve with Toaft.

Water-Mellon. A large Fruit, but nothing near fo big as a Pompion, of a fad Grafs-green, the Seeds are black, the Pulpe exceeding juicy. It is often given for Heat and Thirft in Feavers and other hot Difeafes with good Succefs.

Brown

Brown Take two Quarts of Water
Caudle. and mix it with four Spoonfuls
of Oat-meal, a Blade of Mace and a
Piece of Lemon-peal. Let it boil, and
keep ftirring it very often. Let it boil
a Quarter of an Hour, and be careful
not to let it boil over; then ftrain it
through a coarfe Sieve. Add a Quart
of Ale that is not bitter. Boil it and
then fweeten to your Tafte, and add half
a Pint of white Wine or Brandy.

Cold Boil a quart of Spring Water;
Caudle. when cold add the
yolk of an Egg, the juice of
a fmall Lemon, fix Spoon-
fuls of fweet Wine, Sugar
to your Tafte and Syrup of Lemon one
Ounce.

Of

Of Sundry Other Things.

Candle making. The wicks of Candles fhould be made of Cotton and fome have thought it Advantageous to fteep them in Lime - water, in which there has been confiderable Saltpetre diffolved. It is of the utmoft Importance that 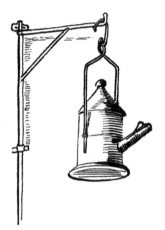 your wick fhould be of the right Proportion to the material of which your Candle is compofed.

Wax Candles. Soften and work the Wax in a Kettle of warm water; then take it out in Pieces and bit by bit difpofe it round a Cotton Wick flightly twifted, which is hung upon a Hook in the wall, beginning at the bottom and proceeding up. The Hands fhould be rubbed with

Olive

Olive oil or Lard. When the Candles are large enough make them Round and Smooth by rolling them on a Table with a board that is kept moiftened by hot Water.

Dipped Place the Wicks a fhort Dif-
Candles. tance apart over your rods, and when your tallow is melted and fkimmed, dip the Wicks into it, taking care that they do not Stick together. Hold them over the Pot a moment to drain, and then Place the rod acrofs the Backs of two chairs. Other Rods may be dipped now, and by the time you have been the Rounds the firft ones will be Hard enough to dip again. Repeat this until the Candles are of the defired thicknefs. During the procefs your pot will probably have to be fupplied with frefh hot Tallow. But not too Hot, or it will melt that already formed on the wicks.

Mould

Mould Pewter can-
Candles. dle moulds are
now made, with an
Aperture at the bot-
tom, through which
the wick is Paffed and
brought up to the top
where it is held in Place
by a fmall ftick. The
wicks adjufted, the Tal-
low is Poured into the
mould and allowed to
Harden.

To make Take a quantity of rufhes dur-
Rufh ing the Seafon, and ftrip off the
Lights. Skin from two fides, leaving the
Pith bare ; thefe being quite Dry, dip
them in melted Greafe repeatedly, and a
good light for all the Purpofes of a Family
may be obtained.

Swarm- Bees when they begin to
ing of fwarm and the Heat of the Sun
Bees. hath drawn them out of their
Hive, do fly about until their Queen
doth

doth by her fitting down determine the Place of their Rendezvous, which they immediately take note of, and all thofe huge Numbers of them do pitch their camp round about their Queen. Prefently after which, a certain kind of Bees, which are called Scouts are fent to difcover Places for them to hive. Thefe fcouts on their return rufh violently upon the fwarm and carry away to the Place which they have found, fome Part of the fwarm, together with the Queen, on whom depends the Unity, good Fortune and Safety of them all.

It is remarkable, that moft Swarms, as foon as they come out, do reft themfelves in fome place near to their old Hives for two or three Hours together, in which time, unlefs they have Hives provided them, they forfake their former Mafter and betake themfelves to the Woods and folitary Places.

But if they have Hives provided, they
fubmit

fubmit themfelves to the Owners of the Hives. The beft Hives are thofe made of clean, unblighted Rye-ftraw. A Swarm fhould always be put into a new hive. Over the Hives there fhould be a cap of thatch, made alfo of clean rye ftraw. The Hives fhould be placed on a bench, the legs of which mice and rats cannot creep up. The common practice of ringing Bells and pans at the time of fwarming is by no means advifable, as it tends to confufe rather than unite your Bees.

Telling the Bees. If you would keep your Bees, in the cafe of a death in the Family, you muft acquaint the little Creatures with the fact either by rapping on the Hives and then faying the Name of the Departed, or elfe by draping the Hives in black and humming in mournful Tune. If you do not do this they will either defert you or die infide of the Hive.

Cookery A few Hints to enable every *for the* Family to affift the Poor of their *Poor.* Neighborhood. At the difcretion of the Miftrefs they can be varied.

A *jug of ſkimmed Milk* is of good Value. When the Oven is already hot a *large pudding* may be made to be given to a fick or young Family thus. Into a deep coarfe Pan put half a Pound of Rice, four Ounces of coarfe  Sugar or Treacle, two quarts of Milk and two Ounces of Scraps or top-pot, fet it cold in the oven. It will take a good while to be enough.

A very good Meal may be beftowed in a thing called *Brewis,* thus made. Cut a very thick upper cruft of Bread, and put it in the Pot where falt beef is near ready : it will attract fome of the Fat, and when fwelled out, will be quite a delect-able Difh to thofe who rarely tafte Meat.

Soups. The Cook fhould fave the boiling of every piece of Meat, Ham and Tongue, however falt, and by adding

Bones, barley, the Trimmings of the Vegetables and the odds and ends other-wife wafted, and by putting them on as foon as the dinner is ferved, to fave a fecond fire, very nutritious Soups for the laborious Poor can be obtained, affording them better Nourifhment than they would otherwife get. What a Relief to the labouring Hufband inftead of Bread and Cheefe, to have a warm comfortable Meal! to the fick, aged and infant branches how important an advantage! nor lefs to the induftrious Mother, who often forbears that others may have a larger Share.

To Ex- So many fatal Accidents arife *tinguifh* from light Dreffes catching Fire *Fire in* no Manual for Females is com- *Female* plete without the following cau- *Dreffes.* tions.

1*ft.* Let every Female mind be im- preffed that Flame tends always upward : that fhe will burn more rapidly if up- right than if laid on the Floor.

2*nd.*

2nd. Give inftant Alarm by fcreaming or pulling the Bell, (which is ufually near the fire-place), but if poffible avoid opening the door.

3rd. The Alarm fhould be given while the Female is rolling in the rug, tearing off the burnt clothes, or turning her clothes over her head.

4th. A Man may quickly ftrip off his coat and wrap it around a Female.

5th. If the Victim cannot fave herfelf entire, let her protect her bofom and face by croffing her hands and arms over thefe Parts.

6th. A Piece of green or fcarlet-baize called a Fire-extinguifher fhould be in univerfal Ufe in Sitting-Rooms and Nurferies, and its Name and ufe known, although it ferve as a Table or Piano-forte Cover.

7th. Let the injured Perfon have cold Water plentifully pored over them if they cannot be immerfed in Water till Medical Advice is obtained.

Hints

Hints for Gentlewoman at Table. A Gentlewoman being at table abroad or at home muſt obſerve to keep her Body ſtraight, and lean not by any means

with her Elbows, or by ravenous Geſture diſcover a voracious appetite; talk not when you have Meat in your Mouth; do not ſmack like a Pig nor venture to eat ſpoonmeat ſo hot that the Tears ſtand in your Eyes, which is as un-ſeemly as the Gentlewoman who pre-tended to have as little Stomach as ſhe had Mouth, and therefore would not ſwal-low her Peas by Spoonful, but took them one by one and cut them in two before ſhe would eat them. It is very uncomely to drink ſo large a Draught that your Breath is almoſt gone, and are forced to blow ſtrongly to recover yourſelf, throwing down your Liquor as into a Funnel is an Action fitter for a Juggler than a Gen-tlewoman. In carving at your own Table diſtribute the beſt Pieces firſt, and it will

appear

appear very comely and decent to ufe a Fork; fo touch no piece of Meat without it.

To fit Cloth for Dyeing. Take all the Greafe from your Cloth by wafhing with Pearlafh and Soap, in foft Water, afterwards rincing thoroughly, and put into the Dye while ftill moift.

Ufe a Brafs or Copper Kettle, fcoured very bright, and ftir the Goods conftantly while in the Dye. Moft Goods fhould be paffed directly from the Dye into clear Water and rinced feveral times and hung up without wringing. It is beft to prefs them before any Part becomes dry.

Nankeen Die. Boil equal Parts of Annatto and common Potafh in Water till the whole is diffolved; this will produce the pale reddifh Buff fo much in ufe and fold under the Name of Nankeen Die.

To

To Dye   The Scarlet muſcle found near
Scarlet. Boſton   hath   a   purple   Vein,
which being prickt with a Needle yieldeth
a perfect ſcarlet Juice, dying Linnen ſo
that no waſhing will wear it out, but keeps
its Luſtre for many Years.   Handker-
chiefs and Shirts are marked with it.

To Die   Let   the   Twiſt   or   Yarn   be
Cotton   boiled   in   pure   Water to   cleanſe
a Fine   it;   then   wring   it,   and   run   it
Buff.   through   a   diluted   Solution   of

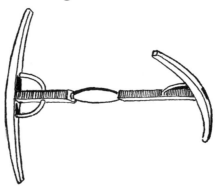

iron Liquor : wring and run through lime
water to raiſe it; wring it again, and run
through a Solution of Starch and Water;
then wring it once more and dry, wind,
warp, and weave for uſe.

Dreſſing Flax to Reſemble Silk. Tie Handsfuls of flax at both Ends to prevent its tangling, but ſpread out the middle as much as poſſible, place in a Kettle, the Bottom of which has been covered with Straw; cover Flax with Cloth, then continue, covering each Layer of Flax with Cloth, until the Kettle be nearly full. Pour over a clear Lie of one part Lime and two

parts wood Aſhes, with due proportion of Water. After boiling ſome hours take out and throw into cold Water. The Flax muſt be then dried, hackled, beaten and rubbed Fine; and dreſſed firſt through a large comb, then through a fine one. By this proceſs the Flax acquires a bright and ſoft Thread.

Soap. In the city, I believe, it is better to exchange Aſhes and Greaſe for Soap; but in the Country, I am certain, it is good Economy to make one's own Soap. If you burn Wood, you can make your own Lye; but the aſhes of Coal is not worth much. Bore ſmall Holes in the Bottom of a Barrel, place four Bricks around, and fill the Barrel with Aſhes. Wet the Aſhes well, but not enough to drop; let it ſoak thus three or four Days; then pour a gallon of Water in every hour or two, for a Day or more, and let it drop into a Pail or Tub beneath. Keep it dripping till the color of the Lye ſhows the ſtrength is exhauſted. If your Lye is not ſtrong enough, you muſt fill your Barrel with freſh Aſhes and let the Lye run through it. Some people take a Barrel without any bottom, and lay ſticks and ſtraws acroſs to prevent the Aſhes from falling through. To make a Barrel of Soap, it will require about five or ſix Buſhels of Aſhes, with at leaſt four quarts of un-ſlacked Stone Lime; if ſlacked double the quantity. When you draw off a part of the Lye, put the Lime (whether ſlack

216   or

or not) into two or three Pails of boiling Water, and add it to the Aſhes, and let it drain through. Three pounds of Greaſe, ſhould be put into a pailful of Lye. The great Difficulty in making Soap 'come,' originates in want of Judgment about the Strength of the Lye. One Rule may be ſafely truſted : If your Lye will bear up an Egg, or a Potato, so you can ſee a piece of the Surface as big as ninepence, it is juſt ſtrong enough. If it ſinks below the top of the Lye, it is too weak, and will never make ſoap; if it is buoyed up half-way, the Lye is too ſtrong, and that is juſt as bad. A bit of quick-lime, thrown in while the Soap is boiling is of ſervice. When the Soap becomes ropy, carry it down cellar in Pails and empty it into a barrel. It takes about twenty-four pounds of Greaſe for a Barrel of Soap.

217 *To*

To Pre- No young Female fhould con-
pare template Matrimony until fhe
Herbs has learned the ufe of the Simples
and
Simples. that grow at her door. For all
the Difeafes of a Locality there
is a remedy provided if we have the wit
to find it. Apothecaries make a very
great profit on the Sales thereof, and if
you have them not you can go Simpling
on the road fide in Auguft and gather all
you will, only be fure
that the day be Sunny
and the Herb is in the
full of its Bloom, not on
the Wane. Many Sim-
ples are good as Pot-
herbs, and the fame Rule governs both.
Let them be dried in a Dutch Oven before the fire, then ftalk them and bray
them in a Mortar to a Powder, put them
in open mouthed Bottles and Label them,
it is much tidier than tying them in
Bunches. Among the Savoury Herbs,
the Bafil, marjorum, Thyme, Sage, Mint,
Rofemary, Summer Savoury and Saffron
are the moft ufeful. The Simples in all

well

well ordered Houſeholds, are Penny-royal, Rue and Hyſſops, Elderblows, Thoroughwort, Smartweed, Motherwort, Worm wood, Burdock and Horſe radiſh Efficacious as Drafts. Sweet Balm and Pepper boiled with milk is a rare vapour for a quinſy. Theſe are generally prepared as Ptiſans.

To take Care of Board Floors. After waſhing very nicely with Soda and warm water, bruſhing them the way the Boards run, dry with clean Cloths, rubbing hard the ſame way. The Floor ſhould not often be Wetted, but once a week dry rubbed with hot Sand. It makes a very pretty Floor to lay the Sand on in a Pattern.

What

What Provisions to take on a Journey at Sea. To thofe who have the inclination for the Voyage, I would commend a few Lines from the pen of Experience. Although every Man have Ship-provifions allowed him for his five Pounds a Man, which is falt Beefe, Porke, falt Fifh, Butter, Cheefe, Peafe, Pottage, Wattergrewell, and fuch Kind of Victuals, with good Bifkets and fixe-fhilling Beere; Yet will it be neceffary to carry fome Comfortable Refrefhing of frefh Victuall. As firft, for fuch as have Ability, fome Conferves, and good Claret Wine, for fuch as are feafick, Sallet - oyle, likewife Prunes are good to be ftewed. Sugar for many things; White Bifkets, and Egges and Bacon, Rice, Poultry, and fome Weather Sheepe to kill aboard the Ship: and fine floure-baked Meats, will keepe about a Weeke or nine Days at Sea. Juice of Lemonds well put up, is good either to Prevent or Cure the Scurvy. Here it muft not be Forgotten to carry

Skillets

Skillets or Pipkins and fmall Frying-pans, to drefs their Victuals in at Sea. For Bedding, fo it be Eafie and Cleanely, and Warme it is no Matter how old or coarfe it be for the ufe of the Sea, and fo like-wife for the Apparell, the oldeft Clothes be the fitteft, with a long coarfe coat, to keep better things from the pitched Ropes and Planks. Whofoever fhall put to Sea in a Stoute and well-conditioned Ship, having an honeft Mafter and loving fea-men fhall not neede to feare, but fhall find as good Content as on Land.

Plaiting In the Country where Grain *Straw.* is ufed it is a good Plan to teach Children to prepare and braid Straw for their own Bonnets, and their brothers Hats. It is an elegant and ufeful Ac-complifhment.

Fans Where Turkeys and Geefe *and* are kept, handfome feather Fans *Wings.* may as well be made by the younger Members of the Family as to be bought. Never throw away Wings of

fowls

fowls, they are moft ufeful. Even the left-hand wings are ufeful to Ambidexters or left-handed People.

Odd In this Country we are apt to
Scraps let Children romp away their Ex-
for the iftence in ufelefs play. This is
Econom-
ical. not well either for
the purfes and
Patience of Parents, or the
Morals and Habits of
children. They can make
Mats for the Table and
Mats for the Floor. They can weed the Garden, pick Cranberries from the Medow to carry to market, and they can Drive the Cows.

Patch- It is indeed a foolifh Wafte
work. to tear Cloth to bits for the
Sake of arranging it anew in fantaftic Figures, but *Patchwork* is good Econ-omy when a large Family may be kept out of Idlenefs and a few Shillings faved by thus ufing fcraps of Gowns, Curtains and fo forth.

Picking Black-berries. Provided Brothers and Sisters go together, and are not allowed to go with bad Children, it is better a great deal for the Boys and Girls to be picking Blackberries at six cents a Quart than to be wearing out their Clothes in senseless Play. They enjoy themselves just as well, and are earning Something to buy Clothes at the same time they are tearing them.

Knitting. Stockings should be knit at Home, as they wear twice as long as woven Ones, and can be done at odd Moments which otherwise would be wasted. Where there are Children or aged People it is sufficient to recommend Knitting that it is an Employment.

To

To Warm Beds. Take all the black or blazing Coals out of the pan, and fcatter a little falt on the remainder. This will prevent the Smell of fulphur, fo difagreeable to delicate perfons.

Method of Tak-ing Profiles. Pafte on Glafs of fufficient Size, a Sheet of very thin poft Paper, which has been well oiled to render it more tranfparent. Erect this in fome Manner fo that it is Stationary. Place the Perfon whofe Por-trait is to be taken in an Arm Chair, with Glafs next the Face. The Light ufed muft be Brilliant and very Steady. A patent Argand Lamp being better than a Candle if to be obtained, but a large Candle will anfwer the Purpofe. Place as near the fubject as poffible, then draw on the Paper on the other fide of the Glafs, with a fine black Lead pencil, the out-line of the fhadow; when fin-

ifhed

ifhed to be transferred by Tracing to other Paper. The beſt Method of Reducing Shades is by a pentagraph, tho' a Perſon who has any knowledge of Drawing may do very well by the Eye or by the method of ſquares, which is uſed in reducing large Pictures.

Black Ink. Take a Gallon of Rain or ſoft Water, and three Quarters of a Pound of blue galls bruiſed ; infuſe them three Weeks, ſtirring them daily. Then add four ounces of green Copperas, four Ounces of Logwood-chips, ſix Ounces of gum arabic, and a wine glaſs full of Brandy.

Sympathetic Ink. Write with an infuſion of galls, and when the writing is required to appear, dip it into a ſolution of ſulphate of Iron ; the Letters will appear Black.

To make Red Sealing Wax. Take of Shell-lac well-powdered two parts, of Refin and Vermilion, powdered each one part. Mix well and melt them over a gentle fire, and when thoroughly incorporated Work the

Wax into Sticks. Where Shell-lac cannot be procured, take Seed-lac.

To make a Sweet Bag for Linen. Take a Pound of Orris-roots, a Pound of fweet Calamus, a Pound of Cyprus-roots, a Pound of dried Lemon-Peel, a Pound

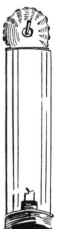

of dried Orange-peel, a peck of dried Rofes, make thefe into a grofs Powder; Coriander-feeds, four Ounces, Nutmeg One Ounce and half, an Ounce of Cloves; Make all thefe into fine powder and mix with the other; Add Mufk and Ambergreafe, then four large Handfuls of Lavender-flowers, a Handful of Sweet-marjoram, a Handful

of

of Orange-leaves, a Handful of young Walnut-leaves, all dry'd and rubbed; mix all together with fome bits of Cotton perfumed with Effences, and put in Bags to lay in your Linen.

Expeditious Method of Diftilling Simple Water. Tie a piece of Muflin or Gauze over a glazed earthen Pot, whofe Mouth is juft large enough to receive the Bottom of a warming Pan, on this cloth lay the herb, clipped, then place upon them the warming pan of live coals, to caufe heat, juft enough to prevent burning; the Steam iffuing from the Herb muft defcend into the Pot, and collect into Water.

Native Ground Books & Music

Books of Songs, Instruction & Lore

Backpocket Bluegrass Songbook
Backpocket Old-Time Songbook
Banjo for Complete Ignoramus!
Bluegrass Gospel Songbook
Bluegrass Mandolin Ignoramus!
Clawhammer Banjo Ignoramus!
Cowboy Songs, Jokes & Lingo
Flatpicking Guitar Ignoramus!
Front Porch Songs & Stories
Outlaw Ballads, Legends, & Lore

Old-Time Gospel Songbook
Railroad Fever
Rousing Songs of Civil War
Log Cabin Pioneers
Rural Roots of Bluegrass
Southern Mountain Banjo
Southern Mountain Fiddle
Southern Mountain Guitar
Southern Mountain Mandolin
Southern Mountain Dulcimer

Recordings

Authentic Outlaw Ballads
Ballads & Songs of Civil War
Bullfrogs on Your Mind
Cowboy Songs
Front Porch Favorites
Love Songs of the Civil War
The Home Front
Log Cabin Songs

Old-Time Gospel Favorites
Raccoon and a Possum
Railroadin' Classics
Railroad Fever
Singing Rails
Songs of the Santa Fe Trail
Southern Mountain Classics
Southern Soldier Boy

Old-Timey Cookbooks

A Garden Supper Tonight
1st American Cookie Lady
Children at the Hearth
Mama's in the Kitchen
Old-Time Farmhouse Cooking
Log Cabin Cooking

Lost Art of Pie Making
Pioneer Village Cookbook
Secrets of Old-Timey Cooks
Take Two and Butter 'Em
　　While They're Hot!

Write or call for a FREE Catalog
Native Ground Books & Music
109 Bell Road
Asheville, NC 28805
(800) 752-2656

www.nativeground.com　　　banjo@nativeground.com